D0160640

WELD LIBRARY DISTRICT
2227 23rd Avenue
Greeley, CO 80634-6632

DEMCO

An admirable book, full of wisdom, insight, and reaffirmation. Its voice is familiar, and very nice to hear. God and dailiness and sensible thoughtful goodness, side by side in the same sentence.

Sam Waterston
Actor

Raising a Good Kid should be required reading not just for parents, but teachers, religious leaders, in fact, all of us whose lives are touched by teenagers. For this is a book about what it is to be human; made in the image and likeness of God. And who wouldn't want to be made in the image and likeness of the God whom Jack Smith reveals to us. A God who is wise, kind, mysterious, real, contemporary, funny, pleased with the teenagers this God created—and, indeed, pleased with all of us.

The Rt. Rev. M. Thomas Shaw SSJE
Episcopal Bishop of the Diocese of
Massachusetts

As Jack Smith's colleague for twenty-two years, I had the benefit of his voice; of one who understands, indeed affirms, the complexity and uniqueness of each individual and family as well as the forces and pressures affecting adolescents and their parents. With this book a much wider audience will learn from a voice full of insight and wisdom.

William M. Polk
Headmaster, The Groton School

649.125

Raising A good o Kid

(chances are you're doing just fine)

John F. Smith

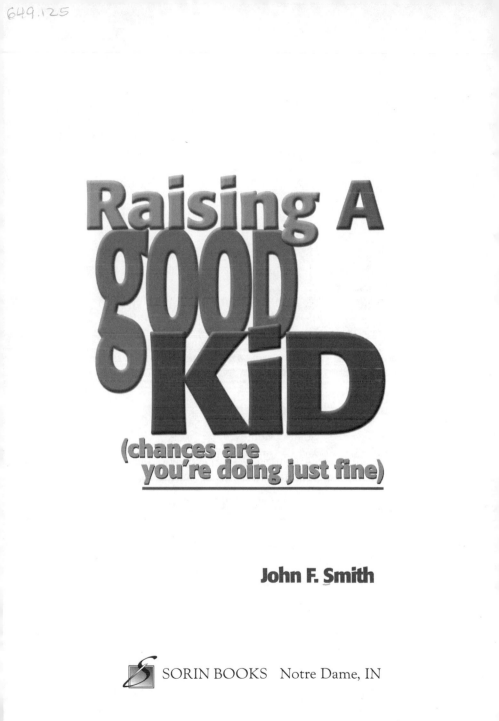

SORIN BOOKS   Notre Dame, IN

WELD LIBRARY DISTRICT
GREELEY, COLORADO

© 2002 by John F. Smith

All rights reserved. No part of this book may be used or reproduced in any manner whatsoever, except in the case of reprints in the context of reviews, without written permission from Sorin Books, P.O. Box 1006, Notre Dame, IN 46556-1006.

www.sorinbooks.com

International Standard Book Number: 1-893732-43-6

Cover design by Brian C. Conley

Text design by Katherine Robinson Coleman

Printed and bound in the United States of America.

Library of Congress Cataloging-in-Publication Data
Smith, John Ferris.
Raising a good kid : chances are you're doing just fine! / John F. Smith.
       p. cm.
ISBN 1-893732-43-6 (pbk.)
1. Parent and teenager. 2. Parent and teenager--Religious aspects--Christianity. 3. Parenting. 4. Adolescence. I. Title.
HQ799.15 .S66 2002
649'.125--dc21

                       2001005305
                       CIP

THIS IS FOR MY

students and colleagues

at Groton School

and Boston University

Contents

"Raising"

a

"At sea" is a good way to describe adolescence. Most kids at times feel tossed around, lost, sometimes overwhelmed by the various demands placed on them. Parents, schools, peers, contemporary youth culture, and their own changing bodies and personalities push and pull them from every direction. Occasionally they perceive markers amidst the seething, heaving waves of life—solid, known virtues by which they can set a course, their own course. Sometimes this might be in defiance of what they've been taught; at other times it might be a course that their family, school, or church had advised. A good part of the time kids steer a middle course, one that can at times be in calm waters, at other times in stormy seas perilously close to rocks.

The waters of life are constantly changing, always confusing. Making a successful voyage on them requires courage and risk-taking, qualities that some kids seem to have in abundance, while others acquire them only after considerable effort. But passing through these waters is never an easy task, and it can be fraught with peril. However, pass through them they do, almost all of them, and they sense that the struggle, even some of the senseless struggles, were somehow worth it as they reach the goal of attaining maturity. While this is a lifelong task, it is clear that the passage from childhood to adulthood which we call adolescence is one of the most crucial periods of life.

One of my favorite students told me how foolish he sometimes felt when he contemplated the last few years as he came into his own. "And the worst thing is that you realize, almost every time, your parents were right. I hate that!" He stopped and thought for a while, then he looked at me and grinned. "But it was a helluva lot of fun, anyway." He was lucky to be bright, athletic, funny, good-looking, and reasonably well-off, but he was most fortunate to have parents who were committed, loving, attentive, honest, and above all, trustworthy. They raised a good kid.

This metaphor of the sea is not unknown to us. The Bible speaks of God moving across waters, of God's presence in a storm, frightening, even dangerous. There God can be a source of challenge, even trouble, in the sense of raising possibilities and stirring our consciences, breaking through our self-centeredness, our sense of privilege, our smugness, moving us into an unknown future. God's voice crashes over the roar of the wind and the sea,

calling, rebuking, supporting us, speaking directly
to our hearts and minds.

> The voice of the Lord is upon the waters; the
> God of glory thunders;
>
> the Lord is upon the mighty waters.
>
> The voice of the Lord is a powerful voice;
>
> the voice of the Lord is a voice of splendor.
>
> *P s a l m   2 9 : 3 - 4*

The Bible also speaks of God's presence, the
Spirit, the breath of life, moving across the waters as
the source of creation (Gn 1:1-2). God's Spirit also
brings wisdom, profound understanding of the self,
the self as known by God, the true self that we
gradually discover as we pass through life's
journey. This is the same God who is present with
our kids in the storms of adolescence.

God in the storm, God in the stillness. God is
particularly close to those who are "at sea," those
who sail uncharted seas, who struggle to find their
way and reach their destination. We are reassured
in this, for our children's sake. Matthew narrates
the story of Jesus' disciples caught in a storm at sea.
Jesus comes to them, walking on the water. He
reassures them and even invites Peter to come to
him. Peter jumps out of the boat, takes a few steps,
and slips down into the sea as Jesus grabs him and
almost seems to tease him for not being able to walk
on the water, "What's wrong, Peter? It can't be that
hard for someone as sure-footed as you." We do
well to remember God's presence as we sail across
the open waters of life, just as sailors remember to
listen to the weather report and bring their charts
on board when they set out.

Raising a good kid is in the news these days, and many people are happy to tell you just how to do it. It's as if there's an owner's manual for raising a good kid that parents have only to consult in order to press the right buttons, turn the right switches, and produce, at the other end, a perfect child who would roll out all spanking fresh and new, the good kid of your dreams. The owner's manual approach, no matter how tempting, is not helpful because, in fact, it's contrary to everything else we've learned about life. Nothing is ever that certain; there are few flawless ways to approach anything. Almost everything we do, from learning how to read to learning how to operate the latest computer, is done in fits and starts in a kind of educated trial-and-error way. There are people who, when faced with a household task such as installing curtain rods, choosing a new color of paint for the trim, or setting up a VCR or a new CD player have to do it twice. They seldom get it right the first time. Some of this is due to ineptitude; some of it is the complexity of the task.

In fact, what we often find is that the owner's manual doesn't tell us what we really need to know, or it conveys information in a garbled manner. I discovered a button on my rather complicated camera the other day, the use of which was a mystery to me. When I consulted the owner's manual I found that there was no entry for that button. Sometimes we are left to our own devices, our own intuition, when solving problems.

In this book I am proposing that parents use their own resources, what they intuitively and intelligently know, and look realistically and calmly, even thoughtfully and prayerfully, at the maddening complexity of child-raising. After all, raising a good kid, depending on what you mean by "good" (more about this later), has always been a priority of parents. We have thousands of years of experience doing it. It's true, our historic human experience has not been in this electronic, digitized virtual culture (which we call postmodern), but in general the process of child-raising is one with which we are thoroughly familiar. We were raised once ourselves and we didn't come out too badly, so it shouldn't be too hard to come up with some ideas that might take some of the mystery and, let's be honest, some of the terror out of it.

For many good parents, raising a good kid is terrifying because it is so important to us and because so many things can go wrong. We ache for our children to grow up as well as we can arrange it. Bad examples, kids who are in terrible trouble in one way or another, are all around us; we hear about them on the news and read about them in the newspaper. They were friends of ours in school; sometimes they are members of our family—and it could also be that we ourselves were troubled kids.

Perhaps we can agree that people who say that they are absolutely, completely sure how to raise a good kid have already disqualified themselves from this discussion. After the Littleton, Colorado, high school killings, the papers and air waves were full of experts who were eager to point out that the parents of the young men who did the killing had obviously not had enough contact with them or they would have known that something terrible was about to happen. These critics, some of whom were professionals, none of whom had met either the boys or their parents, knew just exactly why things had gone wrong. It was because the young men had been allowed to grow up in a completely

teenage world, devoid of adult influence. Since
their sons had no significant adult contacts, the
issues of adolescent life had become ultimately
important to them; the gunfire was their reaction to
disappointment and frustration which seemed to
them, in their narrow world, absolute and requiring
an absolute solution. That was it; the solution was
that parents should be involved with their children.
(Homer Simpson would say, "D'oh!")

About two months after the horrible incident, a
national newspaper printed a long article based on
extensive interviews and discussions with members
and friends of the families involved, as well as with
teachers and others who knew them. The
conclusion? The parents were overly involved with
their sons who had reacted against this control. The
solution? Let your child loose to swim in the
adolescent world. Well, that solves it. How do you
raise a good kid? "Be involved with your kid." Or is
it, "Let your kid go"? What's a parent to believe? No
wonder people are confused and upset and seek
unconditional, certain answers to crucial questions.

A scholar recently commented that there is
nothing parents can do to guide their children,
since their world is created for them by their peers.
Of course, we should not underestimate the
influence of peers, or, indeed, the pervasive
influence of modern youth culture—a commercial
culture (of selling) of film, clothes, music, and
sports. But does it make sense to talk about either
total influence on kids, or the complete absence of
it? Children grow up subjected to many kinds of
forces and pressures. They are not just objects or
victims in this world, but also subjects, actors, each
of whom has his or her own unique take on the
world, his or her own reaction to the influences that

crowd in on them. They have to be confident in their self-knowledge, open to the consideration of new ideas, but not victims to the fads that, in our electronic culture, flash endlessly across the screen of our consciousness.

Precisely part of the modern youth culture of which I spoke is the creation of "fads" in clothing, music, and attitude which replace the last fad and require the purchase of new hairdos, new trousers, new jewelry, new expressions of self. We bear with these in young people, knowing that they are trying on and trying out personalities and ways of being, seeking to "find" themselves in the midst of their peers, but there is no reason that adults should be victims of faddish behavior too, especially when it relates to raising our children. No fifty- or sixty-year-old would wear those huge-legged trousers some young men and women sport, neither should we jump at the latest idea in child raising.

For example, not long ago we read that playing Mozart to very young children would help develop the thinking part of their brains. I confess that soon after I read an article about this I bought a CD of the "Jupiter" symphony for my then-newborn grandson, Sam. I like Mozart a lot; to me, his music is full of life, of good ideas, of joy. The great Protestant theologian Karl Barth apparently used to listen to Mozart almost exclusively and is reported to have commented that if the angels play Bach for God, then surely they play Mozart for their own pleasure. However, no matter what Barth thought, newspapers recently reported that the studies on which the recommendation was based that Mozart be played for the very young were flawed, that the tests were actually done with college students, and the effect, the "lighting up" of certain parts of the brain, lasted only for a few minutes.

Poor Mozart. We think he would appreciate being the music of choice for children. On the other hand, if we are going to play music to little children—and it makes sense that if music is pleasurable for adults, usually for reasons we don't understand, then it is for children also—then why not play Mozart? I can't imagine a baby going to sleep listening to "heavy metal," but it is conceivable that Mozart would put a child to sleep in equally as good a humor as he puts me to sleep. So keep on playing the Mozart, but forget about creating geniuses with your CD player.

Parents might well be skeptical about analysts and "experts" who seem to know little or nothing about the specific situation they address. Beyond that, they might well think that those who assert that they possess the magic pill, the essential technique, the correct attitude, the secret knowledge that will make everything turn out right for all children, have seriously oversimplified the issue. After all, it's nothing more or less than one of the questions that has plagued and puzzled human beings forever: how to help children grow up, how, for example, to maintain each one's uniqueness while living in community and in a mass society. The fact that we haven't come up with a sure-fire program after raising kids for many thousands of years might lead us to conclude there isn't an absolute or easy answer.

In forty years of living and working with young people, I've known many families who have had troubled children, and may others who have had so-called successful children. However, the experience of each family was so special, so specific to the particular situation that an honest person would find it hard to say, "This is what they did that made things go wrong," or conversely, "This made everything come together." The one-size-fits-all approach might be all right for socks but not for people. Parents are sometimes so intimidated by professionals and others who offer sure solutions that they don't trust themselves to know their kids and what actually went on in their family. After all, what actually did happen as someone grew up is what is crucial to understanding the situation, not what a consultant thought must have happened, or even what a member of the family "feels" happened. Feelings are important and need to be taken seriously, but they are not facts. It seems to me, in accord with many others, that if someone feels a certain way, it is not an indication that events occurred, but simply tells us that they feel a certain way.

I don't think child-raising is a matter of being conservative or progressive. I have known parents whose politics were to the right of Genghis Khan, and parents who were raving leftists with "red diaper" babies. Both sides raised hard working, thoughtful, humane young people. It's something like different teachers. One of the favorite teachers in my daughter's high school was a very conservative young man. At the time, I thought him perhaps a little nervous about being in the classroom with teenagers and needing to assure himself of his control. But my daughter and her classmates appreciated the breadth and depth of his knowledge and his real commitment to their learning. Referring to another teacher, one of my students once said, "There are hard teachers from whom you learn nothing, and there are hard teachers from whom you learn a lot. There are easy teachers from whom you learn nothing and there are easy teachers from whom you learn a lot." She then named a biology teacher, "And there's Mr. B. He's really easy and you learn an incredible amount." Any theory seems to work and any theory seems not to work. It all depends on the chemistry of the thing.

I have known young people who have had horrendous experiences as children and who grew up kind and generous, calm and open in their approach to life. I can think of one whose early childhood was marked by a singular tragedy, the accidental death of a very close sibling. He is as reasonably adventurous as any other young person, sensitive to parental worries, with great good humor easing their concerns, careful not to worry them too much as he makes his way. He is more appreciative of the gradual gift of freedom because he knows how hard it is for his parents to let him go.

I want to disclaim any knowledge of a sure way to create "goodness" in young people. Rather, I want to offer ideas about young people and their growing up, about what values are important, but more about who and what we want our young people to be in the face of the world around them.

We cannot think of young people and families in isolation from what goes on in the country or the world, as if we could create an antiseptic bubble existence for them. We cannot keep them safe, nor, if we think seriously about it, do we want to. If we want them engaged and in relationship with peers and culture, that necessarily involves risk and maybe even a degree of danger. But already we are getting ahead of the story.

Remember also that each person brings to his or her family a past which will be more or less emotionally and spiritually healthy or not, and also that the chemistry of a family is more than the sum of the parts of every member. Some mixtures can be volatile, ready to explode; other mixtures can be placid, composed. While the traumatic events of our past may not be used to excuse our behavior when we do hurtful and immoral things, they can be used to help us understand why we do things, even simple things. Occasionally when my children were growing up, I would say something to them in a tone of voice I instantly recognized as coming from my father. While my father was a kind and loving person, he had his moments, like every one of us. When he was having one of those moments, he would use that tone of voice. It made me angry to hear it, then and now, but especially when I heard it coming out of my own mouth. It was my responsibility to clean up my act. No one can avoid that kind of influence from the past; it is up to each person to understand the presence of the past and its harmful influences, and endeavor not to repeat what has caused pain.

In a talk about his family, a student said that when he was much younger he thought his family must be just about the most normal, even perfect, family. One day his father, who seemed to him a rather young person, took his own life. The young man's wisdom, shared with the students and faculty, and wrought out of years of grief and struggle to come to terms with the event, was that they ought not to think that there were any normal families, and certainly not to expect their own to be perfect. He had recovered his own warmth, kindness, and engaging sense of life, but only after years of painful struggle. (I remember watching him on the dance floor one Saturday night leading the fun while wearing an enormous sombrero,

apropos of nothing but high spirits. I teared up
when I realized how hard-won his recovered joy
was.) It turned out that his father's tragedy would
not be this boy's only adversary, but he has
continued to prevail, garnering the admiration of
his teachers and friends over and over again.

A cartoonist once pictured a large auditorium
with a banner stretched from one side to the other:
"Conference for Children of Normal Families."
Only two people sit in the midst of the rows of
empty seats. All of us go through life with a few
jolts along the way, and find in them concerns that
will strain us to the limit. We all carry in us the
seeds of the tragedies we will find in ourselves and
in our relationships. Because of this, we find in
great works of literature those characters and
families with which we identify and, eventually,
through feeling their suffering ourselves take hope
and heart. If we are not Antigone or Hamlet, we
surely will be Oedipus or Willy Loman's wife. We
learn to prevail, with God's help, through our
suffering and tragedies. In almost all of our
religious traditions we find not a way of avoiding
suffering, but a path of learning from it, taking hope
from it, and coming to terms with it. Jews see their
slavery in Egypt as the precursor of God's mighty
work in delivering them, and Christians
understand the double ending of Jesus' life,
crucifixion and resurrection, as containing promise
and hope. The struggles of Muhammad and
Buddha to understand and prevail, to penetrate to
the mystery of the meaning of existence and
suffering, draw us to see imperfection and evil at
the very least as a condition of all our existence,
something to be faced.

Emily Dickinson's poem may speak to some of
our fears and anxieties about our children:

Hope is the thing with feathers
That perches in the soul,
And sings the tune without the words,
And never stops at all.

And sweetest in the gale is heard;
And sore must be the storm
That could abash the little bird
That kept so many warm.

I've heard it in the chillest land,
And on the strangest sea;
Yet, never, in extremity,
It asked a crumb of me.

Our religious traditions hold out to us a hope that never "asks a crumb" of us, except that we be open to hear the voice of hope. There's no denying that for many of us there will be moments when we are deeply frightened and care-worn about our young people, but hope springs up, it is my experience, in the strangest places and at the strangest times. Teachers learn never to give up hope. They expect that the young person in the corner who is struggling with learning may very well push through the barrier and, precisely because there was a struggle, carry on through vastly more difficult material. Having learned how to study, that person has learned enough about self to adapt to a new learning challenge.

Occasionally, there are students who are so bright and quick that they can easily slip through even very difficult high school subjects without putting in a great deal of effort. However, they miss learning how to settle in and engage with something really hard—grinding out studying, making a topic their own. They become accustomed to the easy way and miss the benefits of genuine challenge, and can sometimes be satisfied with the mediocre, especially as they encounter more and more difficult material. They can tend to doubt themselves, so afraid of risking failure that they do not attempt to be truly excellent. There are benefits where they recognize the need to study hard.

Parents sometimes resent teachers who are "hard" and give their children lower grades than the parents think ought to be given. There are even parents who think their children simply should be given good grades, period. This "entitled" attitude can be quite pervasive. Yet those "hard" teachers, when they are fair and encouraging, are often the ones who are most remembered and appreciated. I know an excellent lawyer who went through school quite easily but remembers one teacher with great respect and affection because "I never had to work until I had Mr. T. He taught me what working hard was like."

It is important to assert that there is some benefit in failure, in not being able to achieve one's goals or conquer some material. If everything comes easy, what happens when the limits of easy competence—none of us are equally competent in every field—are finally reached? Failure has gifts to offer, among them an antidote to arrogance.

A retired teacher at my school used to tell of his most brilliant student, a man so quick and articulate that he could win classroom debates even though he didn't prepare for them. American history bears witness to a time when this man's arrogance, his confidence in his ability to understand without digging deeply, would help to lead the country into a terrible quagmire. While he was certainly not personally responsible for what many regard as an intellectual failure that led to a policy failure, the same attitude shared by those around him certainly was a factor in a great tragedy. In the same way, the arrogant failure to take account of an obscure Islamic mullah named Khomeini led to the disastrous foreign policy surrounding the Islamic resurgence in Iran.

All teachers have also been visited at school by former students who show up cheerful and successful to report that they turned their lives around from what seemed to forecast failure. How wonderful it is to hear, "But you never gave up on me, even when I almost gave up on myself." It's important not to give up, to see even failure and rejection in terms of hope, because they can presage a change, a turning around. That may sound naïve, but experience bears me out. More often than you would suspect, we find that students who leave our schools under something of a cloud return to report how important it was to them that we cared enough to maintain standards of behavior. It dawns on them that in the midst of a chaotic time, the imposition of limits gave them a place to grab onto. If their departure was done correctly, that is, if the school was genuinely sorry about the necessity for a student to leave and communicated that in a firm and clearly worded decision, then the school shared in the student's accomplishment. I know the head of a school who was remembered for years by those he asked to leave—because of his sensitivity and firmness in explaining why, for the extraordinary hope that he communicated to the student. That he could do this at a very painful and difficult moment is a great gift. He enabled a young person to see a future at the moment of failure.

I have visited other schools and by chance met students who have had to leave us. Some of them have done far better than we ever would have dared to hope. Their attitude was usually one of grateful thanks for the hard thing we'd done; they took themselves in hand, gave themselves a good shake, and changed. We let one boy go when he was in the eighth grade. We liked him very much but were convinced he would suffer as a person under the academic competition in our school. I never expected to see him again, but when I preached at another school, there he was, very grown up, a senior, captain of a team, a leader of the student body, and about to attend an Ivy League school. When he told me, we grabbed each other and jumped up and down at the chapel entrance, both of us pleased and excited by the terrific work he and the other school had done. (This was perhaps more noticeable than it needed to be because he's six feet three and I'm five feet six!) This good result out of a difficult decision happens again and again.

Teachers and school administrators relate stories about parents who attempt to create "designer children" who will do everything right because everything right has been done for them. We hear of parents who move children across town to another private school because the third grade in that school has higher test scores than the third grade in the school the child is in. Some parents are unaware that tests can be highly subjective, that scores can vary widely (or that one of the correlations of high scores is the number of times the child has taken the test), or that a whole third grade might have a "bad day."

We cannot, and will not, have perfect kids. In our culture there are people, especially those with financial resources, who attempt to create around their children a perfect world. It's the impulse and expectation for perfection that is so worrisome and so spiritually destructive, leaving nothing to chance when chance is an enormous part of our lives, so much so that some theologians and scientists have called it the true "natural law." The "laws" of nature are nothing compared to the amount of chance, or chaos, in nature; attempts to understand chaotic systems (the weather, for example) have foundered on that chaos. Scientists suggest that the air disturbed by a butterfly's wing in China can cause a system of storms all across the United States over the course of a couple of weeks.

If this chaos is true about the weather, we can be sure it is true about a complicated system such as a family, such as an adolescent. In short, parents should think, work, talk, pray, and do everything they can, but they shouldn't expect to produce a predetermined result in their child. A child raised in a tent by hippie parents may very well grow up to be an investment banker, and the banker's child may take his chances in a rock band or as a filmmaker. Parents may discover that things will not usually come out the way they expect them.

First-time parents may be somewhat dazzled by the uncertainties of parenthood. They should bear in mind that raising a child is a day-by-day enterprise; it is a process that is more like raising crops than creating a chemical compound or assembling an automobile.

When a gardener raises vegetables or flowers, she carefully prepares herself by looking at catalogs, reading about various soils, thinking about adaptability to the weather. She knows what she hopes to grow but is aware that many factors will intervene between her and the finished product. When the right time comes, she prepares the garden very carefully. She even prepares herself for a few disappointments, knowing that there can be a drought or too much rain. When the planting is done, she hovers over her plants, making sure they are fed and watered. She may ask a knowledgeable friend to look at her garden and tell her what she can do to improve conditions. She does all she can do for her garden, but she knows a lot is up to the individual plants, their strengths and weaknesses. She does not pull them up to see how they are doing. In the end, she trusts them and she trusts her careful preparation.

Parents can be confident that their child will grow up into a remarkable and unique person—gradually, slowly, with many a fit and start.

It may be useful to consider the lines from Shakespeare's "The Tempest" (I.ii..394–99), referring to the changes undergone by the drowned father of one of the characters:

> Full fathom five thy father lies;
> Of his bones are coral made;
> Those are pearls that were his eyes:
> Nothing of him that doth fade
> But doth suffer a sea-change
> Into something rich and strange.

We may rightly think of the changes undergone in adolescence as a "sea-change," and hope and pray that they result in something "rich and strange." We all want the "rich" part, that is, a well-rounded, intelligent young person with personality to spare; but we're not so sure we're looking forward to the "strange." Yet there is something strange about each of us. Just as there are no "normal" families, so there are relatively few people that we would recognize as completely normal. We are all quirky in one way or another, some of us are perhaps a little less strange than others. "Strange" is only what we are not used to.

The parents of one of my students brought him to the home of neighbors for lunch. They were very prominent and well-off people. They served their favorite food, head cheese. My young friend thought that was strange! It was a prized delicacy in that house, which didn't help very much.

You can be sure you may not be used to the person your child will decide to be. You may even be surprised when your child becomes something that he or she has decided you would like, when you didn't want that at all. With the parents' support and prayer, a son or daughter will become something "rich and strange," and they will bless the God of all blessings. Their kid will have absorbed from them—more by watching and listening, perhaps when they weren't aware—what goodness they have to offer.

When adolescence has passed and their kid has gone on to another phase of life, the parents may very well discover that they have raised someone even richer and stranger than they dreamed. They would never have dreamed that it is the child they raised who greets them as an adult, comes to their house as visitor, invites them to her or his house as guest, who is so much more competent and confident about life than they could imagine. James Joyce wrote about the boys in Stephen Dedalus's school, "And every single fellow had a different way of walking." If parents have raised good kids, they will hope that every single one of their children will have a different way of walking through life—and they will thank God for it.

A
" good " KiD ?

When we say "raise a good kid," what do we mean by "good"? We all know young people and, if we are honest with ourselves, we know we make judgments about them, if casually and provisionally. The job of youth is change, so most of us try not to pigeonhole kids as "good" or "bad." We are aware that the child who acts out family problems or comes under the influence of "bad" kids will likely clean up his or her act as part of the long process of learning and growing into his or her identity. There are some popular kids we find hard to like. Do we sense that they are manipulative, like Eddie Haskell in *Leave It to Beaver*, or are they merely boring? Some kids we can't help liking even as we hope they move through the adolescent willy-wobbles quickly and get themselves together. While "liking" is not really the most useful tool in dealing with deep issues of selfhood, we have an intuitive sense that we tend to like "good kids."

This tends to make us suspect that being a good kid is more than being ethically "good." Our notion of what makes someone a "good" person in a profound and spiritual sense includes the ethical, but moves through it to questions of meaning and purpose, of authenticity of the self, being the person one was meant to be, doing the hard spiritual work of being oneself before God, having what Søren Kierkegaard called "purity of heart."

I would suspect that by "good kids" few people mean "goody-goody," referring to a priggish young person who has isolated him or herself from life to preserve the kind of political, moral, or spiritual purity that can be maintained only in separation from ordinary people and ordinary life. This would be a perversion of the notion of "good," even of the notion of "pure," which we could think of as intensity of purpose in the midst of distraction, straightness of conduct in the midst of ambiguity.

We have a healthy tendency, I think, to know that there is no one without stain, and a healthy tendency to distrust those who are "too good to be true." We want our kids as they grow to be engaged in the rough-and-tumble of the real world of personal, political, and economic activity. We have no illusions about the temptations and ambiguities of those areas. We don't want kids to be so afraid of being wrong or getting their hands dirty that they don't do anything. We don't want them to shirk risk-taking because they might possibly make a mistake. Everyone does things that are, in retrospect, wrong. Not many of us set out deliberately to hurt, cheat, or deceive, but at the same time most of us are appalled at some of the things that we have deliberately or inadvertently done or contemplated doing. Parents who have truly high moral standards also understand that no one is perfect. It seems to me that the adoption of serious values involves an understanding, if not an acceptance, of human imperfection. Maintaining high standards of conduct includes the possibility that at some time, unfortunately, those standards will be violated. Good parents make provision for that eventuality; they know what their reaction will be to acts that fall below the level of acceptability. They are ready to confront their children calmly about unethical acts and respond in appropriate ways.

There is no contradiction or hypocrisy in knowing what is right, trying to do it, and failing. Understanding that one will almost inevitably make mistakes and do stupid things doesn't mean that they aren't either mistakes, stupid, or wrong. The young man referred to earlier in this book who said he hated it when his parents were right, but that they always were, was described by his roommate in this way: "I don't understand how someone who is so smart can do so many dumb things." But we do understand this; it is called being human, part of growing up. One reason why we all liked this young, smart doer of stupid things was that he could admit his mistakes openly and with good humor, a good kid. All of our religions affirm the universality of human failing; all make provision for dealing with it.

Our relationships with young people should make provision for failings, while making it clear that the family is committed to a moral standard. Although the world is difficult and ambiguous, it must also be said, and said clearly and unambiguously to children, that there are things that are always right and things that are always wrong. For example, it is, I think, always right not to be deceptive, to be truthful and honest. It is always right to respect the dignity of others and their property. It is right to be trustworthy in our relationships with others. It is right to identify with others' experiences and to learn to empathize with them. It is right to be open and generous to all people. It is right to do what one can for the common good. These instances may not be "cool" in our cynical world, but many of us would agree that even if everyone in the world voted for lying, hatred, prejudice, and greed we would still say they were absolutely wrong. Many Germans voted for Hitler and the Nazi party; this does not change for a moment that the ideas of the Nazis, their deification of the national state and denial of the humanity of so many people, were absolutely wrong. I think it's important for parents to stake out clear areas of moral certainty and articulate them firmly. It's even more important for parents to be good examples of good behavior in order to create good kids.

What I have mentioned are some basic moral stances on which every family will expand and develop, interpret in terms of their own ethos and traditions. Later in this book, I will suggest in detail some moral positions that a family might want to consider in order to promote and clarify their standards. In general I think we should go beyond moral rules to basic "habits of being." The citizens of a small town in France famous for their opposition to the Nazis during World War II were asked why they resisted. Their response was not so much that resistance to oppression was the right thing to do as to say, "That's just the way we are. It's our tradition." If we can engage young people in such a way as to inculcate "habits of being," we will have done as good a job as we can.

Our response to relativism—a theory popular with young people who have discovered that there are differences between cultures and ethnic communities concerning the right standards of conduct and who therefore conclude that there is no right and wrong, just different opinions about it— might not be so much to assert rules as to push the discussion forward, to clarify thinking, and above all, to take stands and act on them. It is true that people disagree about right and wrong; some people are monogamous, some polygamous, and both are sure they are right. Does this mean that universal right and wrong don't exist? (One can always ask young people who assert an absolute relativism if they think it would be right to torture children or rape people. Or if they would do it, since everything is relative.) We do a great deal of condemning moral lapses in young people ("Everything's going to hell! In my day, children had some respect!") but do relatively little to make our ideas clear and more applicable to the conditions of our changing world. That is, we fail morally at just the crucial stage of a young person's moral development, not articulating the reasons why an act was right or wrong, not making logical sense out of our moral principles.

Teaching young people morals is less asserting a moral principle (though it is certainly that) than it is in engaging in moral discourse, reasoning and thinking a moral decision through with young people. This is hard work, which is perhaps why we avoid doing it. Young people can be argumentative and provocative, so we have to have patience and wisdom when we deal with them about important issues.

Occasionally we have to remind ourselves that having patience and wisdom is part of the definition of "adult." It is also important to remember that the discussion isn't over when the discussion is over. After a heated conversation in class, a student will often swing by to say, "I've been thinking about what we were talking about the other day. . . ." Sometimes one has prevailed in that discussion, sometimes not. One student who had vehemently and enthusiastically supported capital punishment worked the next summer at a camp for boys in trouble with the law and seriously at risk. He returned to say, "I've been thinking . . . some of these guys don't have a chance . . . there's a lot more to it than I thought . . . it's really complicated. I want you to know I've changed my mind about a lot of things I said last year." A good kid has that kind of honesty, no matter what his opinions. A good kid works hard enough on himself that he can reflect on what he has said in the heat of classroom discussion, deal with a theoretical issue, and realize that the exchange lacked the vital element of reality. He determines what he would do as a person, not just as a thinker and debater. A good kid has that kind of grounding in life.

It is part of maintaining standards of morality that we very naturally suspect people who are "too good," who are "too good to be true." This world is a complicated moral arena; it's easy to offend deeply, even with the best intentions. There are times when there are factors or data not available to us when we are deciding what to do, and thus the acts we perform turn out to be wrong, even though we wished to do only what was right. Good

motives aren't enough; they're necessary but not
sufficient. People are hurt, communities are
crippled, because, like my young friend, even
though we may be smart, we do stupid things. We
have all inadvertently said the wrong thing, blurted
out the wrong word.

Some years ago a friend agonized for weeks
after entering a gallery and automatically calling
out a cheery "How are you?" to the owner she had
known as an acquaintance for years, but who, she
also knew, was suffering from a terminal case of
AIDS, which was obvious in his gradually
deteriorating physical appearance. There could be
no honest or easy reply to her question. Her routine
greeting was utterly inappropriate in a non-routine
situation. Her real concern for him was drowned in
a careless greeting which in his case had no possible
cheery response. We cringe when we think of what
are perhaps trivial, but nonetheless thoughtless,
moments like this.

White people know that we have all been
trained in a kind of racism. No matter how much
we educate ourselves in decent ways of thinking
and acting, there are assumptions and attitudes that
exist in our hearts, which we would be ashamed to
acknowledge in public. Indeed, we are aware that
racism and sexism in our time are less acts of
outright personal hostility (though there are
enough of those to go around) than they are
unacknowledged, unearned, assumed privilege—
privilege that white people, males, heterosexuals
simply take for granted. We go on and on about
weddings in front of our gay friends, at least some
of whom would love to celebrate and solidify their
relationship in that way if they could. We chatter
about going to places where black people would be

made to feel uncomfortable (nothing overt, of
course). We assume that all Latinos like to dance
salsa, or that all African-Americans like rap music
(African-Americans under thirty) or have "rhythm"
or sing gospel music. These stereotypes have
replaced the stereotypes of some years ago, but if
even they are intended more positively they are still
stereotypes. Men assume and make judgments on
the unspoken assumption that all women like to
cook or are interested in clothes and children, that
employment and other opportunities are as open to
women as to men.

One of my colleagues told me how he had done
one of the worst things he could imagine. He had
called one African-American student by another's
name. Perhaps nonteachers will wonder why he
was so upset, but teachers will immediately
understand. He knew that the student would
assume that he thought, "All blacks look alike."
Conscientious, caring, thoughtful about all his
students, he had slipped. He was upset because he
was aware of what the students might think. (Being
teen-agers they perhaps didn't even notice—we are
saved a lot of the time by the sheer giddiness of
teenage life.) Also he was aware that the source of
the "slip" might easily have been an unconscious
racist assumption, a way of looking at blacks as
common to him as to most white people. What
could he do but apologize to the student quickly
and sincerely and hope that he would be forgiven.

The rest of us hoped that he would forgive
himself and continue to be an open, considerate
teacher who meant so much to students. Was he not
a "good" person? He was, and is, a flawed person,
like all of us, trapped in history, living amid social
conditions with deep psychological effects. The

presence of hope in our lives means that we have a
commitment to the future, to ourselves as people of
the future. We hope we will continue to grow and to
become better people than we are. It's important for
us to see teenagers as people in process, and
sometimes a little harder to see ourselves in that
light.

In any case, let's not beat a dead horse. When
we say we want to "raise a good kid," we can't
possibly expect to create a "perfect" kid because
there are no perfect kids any more than there are
perfect people or normal families. The fact that we
and our children are all flawed is a serious spiritual
situation, but not one that prevents us from having
high standards, or acting as well and strongly as we
can in the world, trusting God to have mercy on us
in our bumbling. In fact, we have too many
important things to do, things that are important
for people, to worry constantly about our spiritual
condition. Martin Luther is supposed to have told
his disciple Philip Melanchthon, who had what is
called a "tender conscience" or worrying about
every small sin, to "sin strongly" and to do what he
thought was the right thing, then let the chips fall
where they may. In prep school language, God does
not intend us to be wimps.

We also sometimes lack balance in our
judgments of good and bad. In a conversation with
the parents of one young friend of mine, a senior in
the school, his mother expressed the hope that he
was not sexually active, that he was a virgin. I knew
him as one of the kindest, hardest working,
sweetest young men I'd ever known. He was a
leader, an excellent and passionate athlete, a
wonderful supportive friend, a superb student who
made the classes he was in hum with his purposeful

energy. I also knew that two weeks before, I'd
dropped by his room to ask him about something
and noticed a pair of women's underwear draped
over the end of his bed. (They disappeared when I
turned my head, only to be spotted dangling from
the back pocket of one of his roommates. Such is the
loyalty of young people.)

To concentrate exclusively and make a judgment
on him based on one aspect of his life without
appreciating all the others, which were activities
and attitudes of high moral value, demonstrates, it
seems to me, a lack of a morally balanced
assessment. Of course, one cares whether a young
man or woman is behaving responsibly sexually, but
it might be worthwhile to wonder what it says about
us when sex is the sole aspect of the moral life that
we care about. It's as if the only moral value we care
about is sexuality. One colleague a few years ago
remarked to another that the worst thing one of our
students could do would be to have sex. This left the
second teacher wondering, "What about violence?
What about hatred? What about betrayal?" More
about this later.

I suppose that when many people in our culture
think of a "good kid," they think of a young person
who is "successful." If one follows the usual
standards of "success" in our day, this means that
the person is economically well-off. A "good" kid is
a kid with a lot of money and property, a
"respectable" person. In this way we reduce our
human vision and dream to economics. (Any
number of people have noted that Western
capitalists are as materialistic, perhaps more so,
than the communists whose philosophy was,
after all, at least called dialectical materialism.
Considering that communism, or what passed for

communism, has almost disappeared, the field
seems clear for capitalism as the new true and only
religion, one that celebrates individualism as its
highest good and possessions as its gods. It is just
this tendency in the West which has been criticized
so severely by Pope John Paul II.) Is it not true that
there is a tendency in our culture, either consciously
or unconsciously, to evaluate human life by how
much a person makes or owns, to the exclusion of
every other value? Is this worthy of a people of
whom the psalmist wrote that they are "a little
lower than the angels"?

We maintain that we are a people of spiritual
values, but an honest look at our values might
indicate that they are responsive largely to the spirit
of acquisition, privilege, and possession. It is
possible to forget that there are many kinds of
spirit, some of them not so humane or godly.
Violence and the way we easily rely on it to solve
problems is a spirit infecting our national life. One
quick flip through the television channels will
indicate the large role violence plays in so much of
American life. Consider professional wrestling, a
kind of play-violence that mimics the real thing so
well that many respond to it emotionally as if it
were real. The effects of our attraction to extremely
violent language and acts, even if they are playing
or acting. It makes sense however that rehearsing or
playing at violence doesn't make much of a useful
contribution to young people's lives. It is not too
extreme to say that we "believe" in violence in the
same way that the believer trusts in God. Violence
solves all problems; it is not just the first but the last
resort; we depend on it for our well-being.

It is not enough to be "spiritual"; it is more
important to ask what the spirits are about, who or

what they represent. Theologian and lawyer William Stringfellow used to suggest that we "name the spirits," that we are clear about what sort of spirits we are talking about. He was happy to call much of the spirit of our time, using biblical language, demonic, and named that demon the spirit of Death.

How do we deal with the powerful presence of money as a sign of "success," and even goodness as a false spiritual value? Many whose lives are economically oriented do in fact draw back at measuring everything in monetary terms. Those who have invested their lives in the accumulation of wealth and property may have many second thoughts. It is a cliché: Faced with death, almost no one thinks, "I regret that I didn't spend more time at the office."

But when we consider the results of this extreme materialism, it often adds up spiritually as identification of wealth and ownership with "winning," as expressed constantly in casual and off-hand remarks about winners and losers. We see that if by "good kid" we mean successful in the terms of our capitalist culture, then we have allowed a very narrow view of human life to overcome the values we believe are more important. It often wins out by default because we fail to articulate values we are convinced are more precious; our values are lost in the clanging of the cash registers.

We know in our heart that monetary success is not the be-all and end-all of life. We are desperate for our young people to care more about becoming persons of integrity, to treat others as precious and unique, to have more interest in decency and honesty than they are about money. We live, however, in a culture that celebrates the accumulation of wealth as the primary goal of human life and makes very clear judgments of people based on this goal. There is a spiritual force in our culture that identifies material success with goodness, that suggests that those who have achieved economic distinction are better, more highly evolved, one would say, than others.

Social Darwinism (a perversion of Darwin as much as it is a perversion of the notion of a good society) is more dangerous for being seldom articulated as such. This assumption, which has been around for 150 years or so, replaces the old aristocracy of birth; this spiritual perversion of meritocracy is part of the walls and floor of our culture. A child can absorb it in the cultural winds that blow through a family home. The notion that those who are lucky enough to have achieved greatly are *better* people than those who have not achieved is as damaging to the spirits of young people in well-off families as it is to those in poor families. A parent might well be on guard against the arrogance that can corrupt the soul of a young person causing, among other things, a sense of "entitlement."

The symptoms of this sickness is that the girl or boy begins to act as if he or she is entitled to, deserves, the special regard and even the service of other people. A teacher at my school spoke of offering the young men in his dormitory a "feed," or snack, of hot dogs. Most of the boys gathered around full of thanks, hungry as all kids are for something to eat late at night. But one boy stood apart from the group with his hot dog and bun in his hand. "I can't believe," he said loudly, "that there's no ketchup for these hot dogs," indicating that the faculty member ought to get busy and provide what he needed, right now! A stiff verbal stuffing and shaking was called for and he got it. A good kid does not feel "entitled," but is grateful when people do things for him and eager to be of help himself, without the expectation of overwhelming gratitude, happy to be part of a community that shares.

It is my experience that many of those who are most successful in the world of finance, the undoubted "winners," are often far from satisfied, and feel a serious lack of fulfillment. Fathers often bitterly regret the endless hours it takes to succeed in, for example, the financial world of New York, which has meant they barely know the children they dearly love. Many of them have feelings of emptiness when they consider their life and what it has been devoted to. They urge their children, for God's sake, as they often say significantly enough, to do something else. Where does it end, this need to accumulate? What are the limits? What will one not do in order to achieve? When is enough enough? Many people who work in finance are haunted by these thoughts, even as they enjoy the fruits of their labor. There's nothing wrong with having money, per se, but sometimes the almost unrestrained pursuit of it can lead a young person into a very difficult and unfortunate spiritual place. Our religious traditions are all concerned with this issue.

Many people find the life of the market and making deals to be almost a kind of game or play, one that gets their blood flowing every day. It is, in a legitimate way, their vocation, or calling. But there are as many who regard the world of their life bleakly, some becoming bitter, cynical, and sad. Let us discuss seriously with our young people the notion that life not only is a process but also has a goal, that there will come a time of looking back and asking what it was all for. The truth is that many people become involved in the money-making world when they are young, with the goal of making themselves rich, or of proving themselves to be worthwhile because they are rich. In time, they find their work unsatisfying and are unable to leave because of financial commitments: mortgages, college tuitions, debts, etc. They realize too late that their wealth proves nothing about them except their ability to manipulate money, and the emptiness they face amid beautiful, luxurious surroundings is part of the pay-off. These are the famous "golden handcuffs" that involve a good deal of tragedy and heartbreak.

What is the conclusion? That money and possessions are not important? It would be foolish and even irresponsible to say that money is unimportant in a world where so many enriching aspects of life are based on wealth, for example, the ability to send one's children to excellent schools and colleges, to expand their understanding and experience through travel. Suggesting that ownership of property and wealth is unimportant trivializes the demonic, death-dealing power of wealth, which comes to possess its owners. Men and women end up serving their money instead of it serving them. It also trivializes the death-dealing power of poverty, which grinds down its victims, depriving them, by distraction, of the spiritual space they need—to breathe freedom and openness, to experience the vastness of the world, and to embrace its beauty in art and nature. It has often occurred to me, for example, that one reason for the general happiness that has prevailed in my life is that my work has allowed me to live in relative comfort in one of the most beautiful cities in America, Boston, and later amidst the rolling hills, apple orchards, and elegant colonial architecture of the town of Groton, Massachusetts. Now, in retirement, I wake in some security each day to walk my dog along an inlet of the Atlantic Ocean, busy with seabirds and a working fishing harbor. These broad views and pleasant surroundings have made for a kind of privilege not experienced by many people. I am grateful for what has been given to me by way of beauty.

The only person who has ever said to me, "Money is not important to me" had so much money that, of course, money wasn't important to her. She assumed its presence, its influence was unacknowledged, and it was certainly unearned. There were a number of people in my school who were in the same situation as this person, so we had a kind of ideology, growing out of the intention of saving young people from being owned by property and possessions, that one ought not to consider money when thinking about vocation. We would often say that, after all, money is not ultimately important, which is true. However, students without money, often people of color, upbraided us for this. "It may not be important for you, but for us, who have nothing, money *is* important, especially since we struggle to make a life for ourselves inside a racist world." Money is in fact important for many reasons and out of many circumstances. It is a good thing to be able to eat what one wants, to go to interesting places, have interesting activities, and support worthy and important causes. Money, in short, creates choices, choices most of us would love to have.

Money is also important, to note the obvious, in maintaining a reasonable standard of living. Religious people have often praised poverty, especially if it is a voluntary poverty, as a superior way of life, but it is important to understand that what was meant by "poverty" in religious communities was having enough, not having nothing. Poverty was a good, it was said, but not penury, not the grinding poverty under which the person can think only of how to survive the next day, not the penury that grinds down the person in the struggle to live, that destroys the spirit and gradually, horribly convinces people that they are worthless.

The questions are: What is enough? What does a family really *need*, as opposed to what does a family *want*? We live in a world in which we have elevated our wants into needs. Some suggest that we live in a culture of needs, where we have decided that we need everything we want. Needs are properly something we cannot survive without. In our culture in very many places one needs transportation, a car. Whether we want a fancy car, the fastest car, the coolest make, or the largest car on the road is a completely different issue from needing a car. What is being given up in order to provide that car? What is being served by its presence? Or, one should perhaps say, whose *ego* is being served by it?

Our needs are broader than we sometimes think. Certainly we need shelter and food. Perhaps it is good food around which the family can gather, share some quiet or loud moments, food that someone—mother or father or young person—has spent some time and effort preparing out of love and commitment to the family. But we also need companionship. A family could serve and teach young children by reaching out to those without companionship, the elderly and the single person, for example. (More later about hospitality as a family virtue.)

Human beings need art, referring to objects and processes that go beyond the everyday. We think of how important music is to young people today, far more than in my youth, and how easily available it is. Rather than complaining constantly about the instruments and arrangements, we might perhaps be happy that they are listening to what are at times, whether older people like it or not, works of art. I am perfectly aware that there are objections to a number of expressions of music and regret music that is violent and misogynist. I also regret music whose sole purpose is commercial and political, created only to pander to the worst instincts of human beings such as acquisition of wealth and hatred of other people. However, relatively little music that young people listen to is actively hateful. And, after all, everything is, as the poet Gerard Manley Hopkins wrote, ". . . seared with trade; bleared, smeared with toil." Like you, like me. We can admit that music and art are produced inside our commercial culture like everything else. When I remarked to a fairly well known artist I know that I had almost talked a friend into buying one of his paintings, he responded in an insulted tone of voice, "It's not a commodity, you know." A gallery owner nearby spoke to me later, "It was for sale, wasn't it?" We have to live, however uncomfortably, inside the world that *is*, as well as hope, pray, and work for the world that *ought* to be.

The arts, and especially music, remain essential needs of the human heart. We should not deny our children the possibilities, the benefits, inherent in them—the possibility of seeing more deeply into the world, of hearing the rhythms of creation, of knowing the structures we share with other elements of creation, of sharing with friends and colleagues the aesthetic contributions of the world and the ethereal visions of the artists.

Besides art it seems to me that a young person needs to experience religious expression. This is important enough that I have devoted a later chapter to it.

We should remember that when the young women textile workers of Lawrence, Massachusetts, went on strike years ago, they sang that they wanted "bread *and* roses," that is, they needed not only the staff of life, but also beauty, art. We admire their ability to think, in a situation of crisis, beyond the immediate and the moment. They remind us that we are indeed fearfully and wonderfully made, that there is far more to this world than that which can be counted or handled.

An important factor in raising a child is the family's moral position or stance toward the world, toward what we might call the common good. A family lives not only in the nexus of parents, grandparents, and their own history but also in a community, actually in various communities, the family, the neighborhood, the school, the church. What a family does in relating to community is far more important than what it says. Over and over again we find children acting out in their lives the values of their parents. On one happy commencement occasion at my school, I enjoyed along with the parents of the graduating seniors a short concert by a singing group. It was the last time many of the youngsters in the group would sing together, the last time their parents would hear them, the last time many of us who were close to them would hear them make beautiful music together. In one corner of the room, a family continued its loud conversation, ignoring what was going on around them and disturbing the occasion for many others. A mother who was standing near looked at me and said, half out-loud, "Rude parents, rude children." If the family were confronted about their behavior I suspect they would have said, "Our child was not involved in the singing group, why should we care?" There's a lot to ponder in that attitude. What is our life in connection with other people all about anyway? What commitment do we have to people outside our experience, outside our family? How much are we willing to limit our pleasure in order to ensure the pleasure of others? How do we as individuals relate to the larger reality of community? What do we owe others? A good kid understands that his reality is bounded by others, that he is touched on every side by them, and that he has a responsibility to feed and help, to nurture the various communities in which he's involved, and which sustain him. Another one of the demons we might name is solipsism, the notion that we are the only reality, that we are not connected to those around us, to every living person. Many of our religious communities would widen that perspective by saying that we are connected through God to all persons who have lived, are living, and who will be living, and to the cosmos. For all of our lives, we are responsible to and for them and for the life of the world.

We can, on the other hand, be overly eager that our children embody what we think of as our good values right now, or at least soon. Growing is a process; it takes time, there are many fits and starts. For example, one of the values we'd like to see in a good kid is a commitment to hard work. We tend to see precursors of the adult commitment to work in school work. But academic work is in many ways not, in fact, a lot like "real" work, work at a job. Parents of young people with learning disorders have learned that low achievement in grades does not mean that a child will not be a hard worker in life. We can make the cruel judgment that a certain young person is lazy or a "slacker," without thinking of what causes this seeming lack of ambition. Many very hard-working and even successful adults have had difficulty in school. Those who spring to mind in this regard are various students, including the children of friends who struggled through school. On achieving adulthood, however, they found that the concentration and focus that escaped them in school were more than abundant when they were at work.

One of my so-so students, someone who clearly had academic ability but whose work was mediocre, graduated and then attended a fine Midwestern university because of his scores and promise in writing. He returned home to stay at Thanksgiving because, as he told his father honestly, "I'm wasting your money." He got a job as a bicycle messenger, leaving his father to think that it would be good for him to discover, in the midst of winter in a northern city, how hard life could be. But this formerly phlegmatic student threw himself into his work with great energy, fighting his way through winter storms and rain. His father was impressed but amazed further when his son came to him to say that he felt he still needed to test himself.

He was determined to go to Alaska to work in
the fishing industry. "All right," said the father,
"but please don't take a job crab fishing." The father
had heard that crab fishing is the most dangerous
and risky of fishing jobs. The son roared off to
Alaska and called a few weeks later rejoicing in
acquiring a job in, you guessed it, crab fishing. After
a good long time, the son called to announce his
approaching return home and asked his father to
help him get reapplication papers to his university.
He was reaccepted, did well, transferred to a school
even more difficult to get in, and is hard at work on
his degree. His father is still a little stunned.

This young man had finally got himself out of
his system. He convinced himself that he was a
worthwhile person in the only way that worked for
him. His father's patience and genuine long-
suffering—we can all identify with the worries of
that fishing season—paid off. We can also discern
that the son had learned somewhere, perhaps from
that stunned and bemused father, himself a hard
creative worker, that hard work, throwing yourself
into something difficult, not easily conquered, and
by sheer grit and application conquering it, was a
path whereby he could find himself. The boy's
teachers knew he was a good kid, though they
wished he'd been more conventionally successful.
In the end, the patience and trust the adults in his
life had placed in him was rewarded. It's important
not to make quick judgments, to think that the
world has come to an end because there is a hitch in
a young person's life, but to continue to have
confidence and trust, as hard as that may be
sometimes. It's important also, of course, to hold up
goals and be realistic about whether they have been
attained.

Change comes at different times for different reasons. One of my students was spotted walking glumly around campus. When he was picked up and offered a ride, he slid into the car in the same frame of mind. "What are you thinking about?" He blurted out that he was thinking what a mediocre person he was. He didn't do well; he didn't do poorly. He was disgusted with his inability really to achieve in his work, but more disgusted with his refusal to commit himself, throw himself into something. I had known his older brother who had struggled with learning. Taking a big chance, I said, "Your brother knows you love and respect him. He really cares for you. You wouldn't let him down by doing better than he did. He knows that the two of you are different people. He wants you to do as well as you can."

The student turned to me, his face clearing. "You're right. Would you let me out here?" I dropped him off and drove away wondering what was going on in his head. Later, he told me that what I had said had suddenly made so much sense that he'd gotten out of the car and gone straight to the academic office to sign up for advanced courses in the field he was interested in—chemistry. He would never have taken that chance before. He did very well in the course, scored at the highest level on the national Advanced Placement tests, and attended one of the best veterinary schools in the world. He became an excellent vet. Not every casual comment had such a remarkable result, by the way. However, in this case, a few moments of thought and a tiny little push at the right time was all it took to turn him into a very hard-working student. He trusted that he was strong enough not only to survive the rigors of the course, to survive not only the possibility of failing, but also to do better than his brother, those two possibilities being the Scylla and Charybdis of his life. Patience and listening paid off. However, we should get it straight: the achievement was not as important as his willingness to risk himself in hard work.

When we say that it's good for kids to learn to work hard, to be challenged, to commit, and to test themselves to tasks that are extremely difficult at the edge of possibility, and that therefore take an enormous effort, we are also saying that it's not good for kids to be "driven," to have their whole identity caught up in the success of the project, or the class grade, or winning the game. If that's all there is, and if the child has caught the idea that the regard of parents is tied up with success in terms of grades, scores, points, popularity, then there will be depths of anger, remorse, and regret that will take a lifetime to deal with. The result may be a restless, driven, never-satisfied adult who is happy to make similar demands of his or her children. Indeed, at least one study suggests that the young people in danger of exploding into violence are not those who are ignored or neglected by adults, but those who are pressured and overscheduled: those who, one might say, have too much adult influence in their lives.

You may think that this is a very narrow path to raising a good kid, this way of demand and not demand. It is. Few of us parents succeed either in modeling it well or describing it with the lucidity required. Nonetheless, the willingness and ability to work hard is a goal worth having when raising a good kid.

A good kid is willing to take risks, to work hard, to recognize that she is not perfect, or that he may take some time to develop, and that he or she may be successful in non-monetary ways. In addition, a good kid is open to other people, devoted to the common good, willing to listen and learn from people who are different. A good kid doesn't think of himself as a finished product, but is curious about who he might become, being secure, and unconditionally loved by his parents. A good kid is free of her parents: free to go her own way, free to enjoy life with them, free to be their friend and even, in some ways, their enemy, but always related to them, for good or ill. A good kid is free to take the risk to feel what other people are feeling, to listen and to watch over people, to care deeply, to feel sad with some, rejoice with others. A good kid laughs at the absurdities of the world, but never at someone in trouble or different from her. She is open to friendship with other kids, protects the weak, does not allow herself to be pushed around, and takes no nonsense. A good kid likes himself and his body, has respect for it, knows that appearances are only appearances. He can look past them to see himself as he really is, and others as they really are.

A good kid is simply the person God has created, living out his or her potential, being who he or she is before God. A good kid is the kid God has more hopes for than any human being could imagine.

The
good KiD
and the Spirit

I t's clear that being a good kid is more than being psychologically healthy, being in touch with reality, especially the reality of feelings; more than being morally healthy, grounded in right and wrong as they affect other people and the self; being physically healthy, taking care of the self and the environment; being intellectually healthy, able to discern and work with the surrounding world. Being a good kid is all these things and more. Essentially it involves being spiritually healthy, being in touch with what cannot be touched, being in touch with hopes and dreams, with setting up a life that has some direction, and not being trapped by the invisible cultural and spiritual forces that tend to imprison us in self-destructive and death-dealing ways of thinking and acting. It means that a young person has a vision of what human life should be and how he or she fits into life. What I mean is better exemplified than described.

When I was fourteen years old, I traveled with my mother to visit her family in Northern Ireland. She hadn't seen her mother or brothers and sisters in more than ten years, World War II having intervened since her last visit. It was an exciting and ultimately very broadening summer for me because I saw first-hand not only that there were people very different from me, "foreign" (George Bernard Shaw's remark about England and America being separated by the same language was apropos), but also that family roots were important and instructive. I learned where all the odd things about us had been generated: why we drank tea, not coffee, overcooked our vegetables, said "bean" instead of "bin" (for "been," however you pronounce it), why we were Episcopalians, didn't like "fusses," and were fairly reticent in the expression of feeling. I began to understand where I had come from and how much difference that made.

And there's the rub. My family was British Protestant, not Celtic Irish, thus they were Unionists who wanted Northern Ireland to stay united with England, not Irish Nationalists who felt the province should be united with the Republic of Ireland. I began to understand my mother's remarks and attitudes about Roman Catholics (always pronounced with a certain twist to the first word), her odd stiffness and forced smile when my friends turned out to be Catholic, or when a cousin dated someone with an Irish name. Nothing was said exactly; there was only that odd stiffness, perhaps a forced politeness that had an effect not exactly intended but unmistakably there. The effect was that there were people who were the "other," the "not-us" who were regarded as "different," but not so that anyone would know. After all, we were not bigots like Northern Ireland Protestant extremists.

I am dissecting here a nearly unconscious reaction, one I suspect that many families share as it is directed at various "different" people. There are times when I have the feeling that I am taking on the role of "other," when I have been in some situations, when I walk down the street with a gay friend, for example. There is nothing wrong with ethnicity or particularity, certainly nothing wrong with family history or tradition, but it all bears a second thoughtful look. Parents particularly will want to ask just what we are saying about ourselves in relation to others when we promote our religious background, ethnicity, or nation of origin. And how can we make sure we are not pushing attitudes absolutely opposed to where we want our kids to be?

My mother would lose her anti-Catholicism only in her nineties when she shared a nursing home room with a Catholic woman of such kindness, openness, and liberality that one could not but be attracted to her. This woman had a spiritual beauty so transparent that there was no resisting her. My mother opened her heart to Regina as she had to very few people in her life. When I came to visit, there was a gentleness, a suppleness, in my mother's relationship to this woman that was immensely gratifying to me. Mother's roommate knew I was an Episcopal

priest, and she took interest in that, but there was
not a trace of the fawning attitude to clergy that
conceals anti-clericalism. She treated me with the
same pleasant irony as, I suspect, she treated her
own pastor. We were not "other" to Regina.
Everyone was "us" and mother melted in her
presence. If someone were to search for the miracle
which is thought to indicate the presence of human
sanctity, he might consider what it takes to heal an
Ulster woman's attitudes to Catholics and think
that Regina was an exemplar of a certain kind of
spiritual charism.

I realize now that at the time of our visit to
Ulster when I was fourteen years old, the summer
of 1949, I was bombarded with all sorts of political
propaganda supporting one side of the "Troubles,"
which at that time would have referred to the
struggles that occurred in the early years of the
century and resulted in the independence of the
Republic of Ireland. Propaganda wasn't all that
bombarded me. There was lots of plain bigotry and
hatred; although in my family it was reasonably
well-mannered, that is, covered up. On the one
hand, my mother's brothers were relatively easy-
going. Both of my uncles, stereotypical Irish
bachelors well into their forties, would go on to
marry Roman Catholic women and father several
children. They lived in a very nationalist town, but
seem to have survived fairly well.

However, my mother's eldest sister's husband,
Uncle Bob, could have been a poster boy on the
Bigotry Calendar's Hater of the Month. His most
famous remark was, "We have nothing against the
Catholic people. It's just that the religion doesn't
make good people." He engaged the depth of
irrationality that not only indicates fanaticism but

also, I think, drives people truly crazy. When he visited, Uncle Bob was typically fond of marching around the kitchen singing anti-Catholic songs. Whenever sentimental people tell me that all music is wonderful because it inevitably brings peace and unity, I think not only of the "Horst Wessel" song, but also what they would think if they had been exposed to Uncle Bob's repertoire of Catholic-baiting lyrics. On a later visit to the United States, Bob turned out to be an equal opportunity hater, displaying his racism or anti-Semitism at the drop of a hat or the sight of an interracial couple.

It was Uncle Bob who that summer took me one day on a trip to a beautiful wooded area, lovely, lush, and green, typical of Ireland. We walked down a path through a wood; it was a kind of country lane on either side of which was a tree-lined hummock. He told me that it was here that a group of Protestant women and children on their way to the local parish church were gunned down by the violent men of the day. This would have been in the 1920s, long before the violence of the present generation.

We walked to the church to view a plaque that listed the names of the victims; over it was printed "Vengeance is mine, saith the Lord." I remember thinking at the time that that was a good thing, that while the act was horrendous, at least the families of the victims had rejected repaying violence with violence, that they had left judgment up to God.

Now I have some further thoughts. What is the real result of suggesting that vengeance must be left up to God? It seems to me that it is to plant in the minds of children—fourteen-year-old boys—the notion that God is vengeful. Think of this: if revenge is one of the characteristics of God, then doesn't it make sense that we should emulate God, embody the characteristics of God? Does it not mean that we should do God's work here on earth? Does it not mean, then, that we should emulate vengeance, a promise and command that my ethnic compatriots and their opposite numbers in Northern Ireland have been taking at least as seriously as any of the other of God's commandments? In fact, it seems to me that the result of the seeming prohibition of violence was to plant the seed of violence, to justify vengeance forever more, and to forge a link in the chain of violence which, despite great progress toward nonviolence, still seems a way of life in some parts of Northern Ireland.

A better way to express the meaning of the Deuteronomy text (32:35) might be to say that in the mercy of God I trust that God will be just to you and to me, as well as to the gunmen and even to Uncle Bob, that the Holy One of Blessing will have more compassion on all of them than they have had for each other.

What this means for us is that we must be very careful when we use language about God before young people. I was lucky enough to be directed in another way, perhaps by my father's commitment to the labor movement, his belief in the dignity of every person. While he shared the casual bigotry of his generation, he was also firm in understanding that discrimination in the workplace, for example, a principle sign of the racism that was endemic on the factory floor, had no true place in a democratic country.

It is easy to communicate twisted ideas to young people, but we should not forget that it is also possible to communicate the truth of justice, dignity, and compassion, to inculcate empathy, openness to the other, and understanding of the other's situation since in this world we seem destined always to be aware of difference and "otherness."

What do we teach young people about God that bends them toward being good kids? I was not taken down that country lane so that I would understand that God reserves judgment for God alone, but so that the idea of vengeance would be implanted in my heart. Who knows how deeply it was set, if it still lives there inside me, ready to be awakened by a casual event or by my diminished capacity. Does it roam my unconscious by surreptitiously forming what I think, teach, and say? God forbid. Casual remarks and attitudes about or toward people who do not share our exact situation, language about God and religion that is not careful and thoughtful can have unforeseen results. We want our children to know God—to have compassion and care for all people, to emulate in their lives that great compassion, and not to learn that God is vengeful and hateful, seeking to reject, and divide us. In places of worship and in family life, parents need to be aware that language which is not balanced, thoughtful, and clear can deeply affect the spiritual lives of their young people.

I recall another event which deeply marked the children of a colleague of mine, a college chaplain. In the late sixties, this family had the privilege of hosting for a week the well-known poet, spiritual leader, and activist Thich Nhat Hanh. They were a little concerned that their house was a typical college chaplain's house, once described by my friend's father as being rather like the post office, "Everybody on campus comes here once a day." It was not the place for a Buddhist monk, who would perhaps require more solitude and quiet than they could provide. However, Nhat Hanh's solitude and quiet was not of the sort that their two daughters, or the extended family of college students and faculty who lived with them and coursed through the house, could disturb.

Every morning their new Vietnamese friend would join them for breakfast. He had brought his own tea, and was pleased when it turned out that my friend knew how to brew it (his English background paid off). The family would involuntarily fall silent as they watched Nhat Hanh hold his mug reverently in his hands, smell the aroma, gaze into it calmly, and then sip gently. They were impressed by how unhurried he seemed, how he allowed himself depth in a simple thing like drinking tea. The frantic pace of life eased a bit in his presence and even my colleague's skeptical wife came to accept the authenticity of this remarkable man.

Each morning of that week when the time came for one of their daughters to be picked up by her car pool, she would stand at the door waiting. She loved school and hated to be late, but the family who were driving that week were invariably not on time. The daughter fretted anxiously as she peered out the window. Nhat Hanh asked why she was troubled and she told him. He nodded, and stood behind her, at some distance, placing his right hand in the middle of her back, sharing his calmness with her, making no demands on her, certainly not telling her she shouldn't feel what she felt. She has never forgotten that quiet presence.

In the same way one of the student residents went for a walk with Nhat Hanh down Beacon Street. The monk simply walked along, but the student was eager for instruction, direction, conversation, instant enlightenment about Buddhism. Finally the young man demanded impatiently, "What are you thinking about right now?" Nhat Hanh responded, "I am aware of the sunlight coming through the leaves." The rest of the walk was carried out in silence.

Nhat Hanh's modesty, quietness, and the mindfulness with which he lived spoke reams about the Great Compassion which he served. Parents of any religion might learn from him and from other Buddhists how we trivialize the holiness of God by our constant chatter about God.

Karl Barth, the great theologian, proposed some years ago that we declare a moratorium on using the word "God" in order to recover the holiness which, for example, Jews honor by never pronouncing the Sacred Name. As we have all noticed, Barth's idea did not exactly take off, and yet the insight is worthy of our consideration. How can kids learn of the mystery and wonder of God if we treat the Holy One as the grocery boy? "Put good weather, good health, happy family, and prosperity over there on the table and close the door when you leave. Oh, and by the way" (fumbling in the pocket for a dollar), "this is for you."

There is a great insight in the Buddhist refusal to personalize that which is the ground of being. This has the effect of preserving the otherness and the closeness which we sense in God. It is an otherness that is paradoxically part of the closeness, the Presence of God. We are, in fact, human and not God, or gods. We do not hold the corners of the world in our hands; we do not stand over history seeing the beginning and end. Sometimes we act as if God is our Uncle Charlie, a slightly eccentric, if well-off, gent who stops in now and again to see if

everything is all right, and who can be counted on
to come around in emergencies.

Anthropomorphizing God can be very
dangerous, as we discovered in Ireland when we
were urged to acts of vengeance because
"vengeance is the Lord's." God is our father, but
God is really not like my father, as fine a man as he
was, nor like yours. We have come recently to speak
of God as our mother—nurturing, creating,
connecting. But God is really not like my mother,
nor like yours. God is unspeakably beyond
whatever good qualities our parents may have.

To speak metaphorically of God is necessary,
since it is the only way we can do so, but it can also
be misleading and dangerous. God is totally other;
our ways are not God's and although God seeks
intimacy with us, we cannot be intimately in tune
with God's will. We must speak about God with
our children, then, most carefully. (We see the
problem when we link the word "vengeance," a
uniquely human quality, with God.) We may not
assume that what is true of us is true of God. God
forbid. But we can assume that what is good in us
is also good in God, but unimaginably more so.
That God is fair and just in ways that go far beyond
our notions of fairness and justice is something I
would like to affirm, and indeed confess, because
God, always compassionate, has been fair and just
to me.

I walked down a country lane in Ireland to be
taught that God is vengeful; my college student
friend walked down Beacon Street in Boston to
learn to be mindful. Parents will help good kids to
learn from the examples of people around them, the
people to whom parents direct them as examples.
("What was it about Aunt Mary that you liked so

much?") Good kids will learn about God and the spiritual life, including the otherness and sacredness of God, as their parents instill those values, those images of God in daily life.

Kids understand when things are being trivialized, and when they are being talked down to. As soon as they discover that this is what is happening, that they have been part of it, or have been regarded as "cute" in their appreciation of religion, they drop the idea like a hot potato. We all hate to be patronized. I have seen students strongly attracted to teachers who seem to relate to them in very personal ways, but they were equally repelled when they discovered that the teacher was manipulating them, taking advantage of their youth, their inexperience, their openness to trust.

Parents who are raising a good kid take care to make it clear that they are not God, who is beyond human description, dwelling "in light inaccessible, hid from our eyes," beyond even human notions of love and justice. God alone knows God. A good kid has a sense of the sacredness of things, of the earth, of his or her self, of his or her body, and a profound sense that these sacred things must not be wasted, polluted, or disrespected because in a way they belong to God. They will understand for themselves the emptiness they feel when people and other sacred things are misused.

Sometimes parents' responsibility to help a child grow in trust of God, to mature faith, will not go as intended. We shouldn't be surprised if our children do not adopt our religious commitments, if they rebel against church and belief as they perhaps rebel against our ideas of what clothing or hairstyle is attractive, what music is worth listening to, what constitutes a proper vocation for them, or who would constitute a good life-partner. If we have done our spiritual work correctly, they will still maintain in their hearts the springing freshness, empathy, and life-giving elan which is the sign of healthy spirituality. And they will respect peoples' spiritual journeys, knowing that there are depths to human life that cannot be described, before which we must maintain a respectful silence, being aware, as it were, of the sunlight coming through the leaves. If our own relationship to God is not profoundly quiet, not expectant and wondering, if it is compounded of rules, demands, barriers, then it is conceivable that our children may rebel, due to the gracious lead of God who wishes to bring them to a better place. The Psalmist says, "All your works praise you, O God." God's work is sometimes resistance, change, and rebellion.

In any case, as I have said before, growing is a process that takes many surprising turns, moving through many stages this way and that before a climactic change or resolution comes.

One young friend was an exemplary student through secondary school and college, graduating with the highest of honors and surrounding himself with good close friends of all kinds. After graduation most of his friends headed off to the city to throw themselves into their careers, positions at Internet start-up companies, training programs at financial institutions, or graduate school. He conceived of spending a summer at a ski resort in the far West, running a ski lift for hikers and mountain bikers. He had a wonderful time on his days off, exercising his athletic talent and resting his mind.

When the fall came, parents and friends expected him to "get started," but he yearned to return to the mountains and live a carefree life doing manual labor for a year. "I know I'll probably end up doing something with my mind, but I'd like to do this just now." I'd never heard that yearning in his voice before. In fact, he'd never asked for anything out of the ordinary, always done superbly what was expected. It occurred to me that so far as I was aware, he'd never asked for something for himself particularly; he was satisfied with what came. So it developed that he needed one detour before the time would be ripe, like the young man who needed to test himself crab fishing in Alaska. Now he's started that journey in a very good way, with the same energy he brought to the mountains, with the same thoughtful mind he brought to his studies. Who knows where he'll end up, but he is all the better for that blissful year on the slopes of the far West.

It was expected, in late nineteenth-century Germany and Scandinavia, that a young person (well, boys) would take some time to "wander," and to discover in that wandering the direction one wanted to go. There's nothing wrong with wandering for a while, and then setting off toward a goal. Eric Erikson was one of the great psychological minds of the twentieth century. He brought us the notion of "identity" and charted the development of personal identity. A good part of our approach to understanding what is going on during a young person's development comes from him. Erikson's personal *Wandershaft* lasted seven years, which seems a bit long even to me. I should say that he didn't actually wander about the countryside ("No, Peter, he didn't follow his favorite band in a van."), but rather tried out various vocations. He did different things, worked in a number of fields during that time. His parents were either very patient or, what is more likely, were helpless to do anything about it. Sometimes we are helpless to do anything other than wait. We then participate in the remarkable patience of God, the patience that God has had to exercise with us.

We might well understand the same thing about our kids' spiritual lives. If we have exemplified meaning and purpose in our own lives as well as we can we can, expect that sooner or later things will come together for our good kids—either in ways that look much like us, or in ways that don't. But after all, they are their own people, and we need to respect their conscience as much as we would respect the conscience and the dignity of any other person.

And we need to respect their need to choose what the will of God is for them. There is a common notion that the will of God is what happens. "It's all for the best; God wills it." "We must accept what happens; we can't understand God's will." In that way, the death of children, terrible natural disasters, even war, have been attributed to the will of God, just because they happened, either through human hands in the course of history or as part of nature. One of my students told the class that the death of his twelve-year-old brother was worth it because it brought his parents closer to God. It was God's way of bringing them to him, the boy said. The assumption was that God must necessarily be interested primarily in people being "religious," interested enough to arrange the death of his brother. He and his parents are privileged to think as they wish, but I could not but wonder at the monstrous God who lived in their hearts, the one who murders children in order to bring people to religious belief.

We know that many accidents are caused by human carelessness, that natural disasters are often compounded by human error or cupidity. Was it the will of God that thousands of people died in the 2001 earthquake in India, or did shoddy construction and political corruption contribute to the natural event? Many cancers are caused by toxic materials in the air or water, but how did the carcinogens get there? When we say that a child's death or the India earthquake was "God's will," then what sort of evil demon are we making of God? The causes of disease, accident, and natural disaster are sometimes pure chance, but there can be a human hand in them as well. It is all too easy and convenient, not to say illogical and untheological, to lay all disasters at God's feet. When we speak of God's will, again, we must be very cautious and not lead an impressionable mind to think of God as the perpetrator of human suffering. We're missing the element of human freedom, for good or evil. The same openness to chance that has a role in human affairs also contains the possibility of free human decisions.

We have brains for a reason; we are free, rational creatures for a reason. A good kid will have a sense of that freedom, that he or she can cool it for a while before leaping into a calling, because the sacred right and duty of young people is to choose their own life.

Jewish people say that choosing a vocation before God is a *mitzvah*, a blessing and an obligation. Parents will allow their sons and daughters the opportunity to make their own

decisions, supporting and listening to them, taking
their decisions seriously because they so want their
child to exercise freedom in responsible ways, and
not in reaction to parental control. There's a fine
line between being supportive and present on the
one hand, and controlling on the other; the
discernment of that line is much more subtle,
difficult, and complicated than it seems. Our kids
deserve our best opinions because we have
experience and maybe wisdom on which our
opinions are built. But that is all we have. Our
children's freedom is theirs alone, and it would be
very wrong for us to attempt to suppress it. We
cannot make their decisions for them. All their
young lives we must prepare them to be free to
make their own decisions, and willing to be
responsible for those decisions, blessing and
obligation inextricably joined.

In the past ten years, teachers have noticed an
increase in parental involvement, some of it not for
the best. It is reasonable that parents are concerned
that their children be treated well, succeed as well
as they are able, be as happy as is possible. It is
unreasonable, however, for parents to demand that
their children succeed regardless of whether they
have mastered academic material or not, that they
be treated differently from other students, and that
their children always be happy, blaming teachers
and friends if that unreasonable expectation is not
met. Life ain't like that, as the man said. Is this not
a vital spiritual issue for parents who have
unquestioningly adopted the standards of success
in a culture that is awash in material goods and
individualism of a radical kind?

I've often suggested to my student friends that
it was a good idea to take a long walk by

themselves, or, if it's summer, a long sail on a calm
day, to give themselves time to think. There are
adult equivalents, including using commuting time
and precious time together as a couple to ponder
what a couple really wants for its children. We don't
take time to reflect, to ponder the decisions that are
ours to make. It's clear that families with more
resources have more choices, but all of us have
some basic choices about directions in which a
young person might go. It's important to utilize
that choice.

Raising a good kid is more of a spiritual task
that it appears. Indeed, if raising a child is not seen
as a spiritual task then we are leaving the task to
others. In that case, it seems to me, we "leave it to
the snake." Being grounded spiritually will bring
perspective and freedom to the task of child raising;
it will give our boy or girl that sense of openness, of
possibility, of decisions being freely made, and of
consequences being accepted responsibly. We are
more likely to be responsible for what we have
chosen than for what we are compelled to do. A
good kid knows this, and accepts the burdens and
joys of responsibility and freedom.

The

good KiD

and School

The boarding school in which I taught for over twenty years is set in the rolling hills of north central Massachusetts, a fairly rural area. Fifty years ago a headmaster who loved nature arrived, and dogs that had previously been banned arrived with him and continue to this day to be almost an essential feature of the place. It is a school where students and faculty work hard and have high expectations of one another. Their work load is known for being formidable. This all creates stress for young people and for faculty and administration.

The parents, like many parents everywhere, are also known for wanting, occasionally demanding, that their children be admitted to the most prestigious colleges, while at the same time not wanting them to feel any pressure or stress. This attitude creates, you guessed it, an enormous amount of stress.

The students of this school for the most part eagerly adapt to the situation. They work remarkably hard, put a great deal of energy into sports and into personal relationships, and throw themselves into extracurricular activities, not only because it's a good thing for college admission but also because they're the kind of young people who "like to keep busy." They are also normal kids who like to kick back and relax, enjoy free time, and who are engaged in all the trials, victories, and defeats of growing up. As healthy boys and girls, they are interested in one another and in experimenting with the various aspects of growing up. As you can imagine, all this energy, yearning, and engagement can also create a good deal of stress, the kind familiar to anyone who knows young people.

But the dogs—lolling around the halls and on the thresholds of the classrooms, waiting patiently outside the dining hall for a student who carelessly carries a cookie back to the classroom building for a snack, dashing off on what seem to us to be pointless errands, playing fighting games with great zeal and ferocious noises, hunting squirrels and never catching one—provide a kind of counterpoint to this boiling energy and ceaseless activity. As a colleague once said wistfully, "Every day is Saturday to a dog." This was said as the teacher was on her way to teach four Saturday classes, coach in the afternoon, and be on dormitory duty that night. Our envy of the life our dogs lived was a constant in our lives and provided a wry and ironic comment on the busyness of our lives.

And yet if one observed the dogs carefully, one could see that our view of a dog's life, which concludes that they are all indolent layabouts needing to get in their twenty-two hours of sleep, is a slander. In fact, there was a good deal of direction to the lives that the dogs lived in the midst of this academic community. This commitment went beyond the usefulness of a dog's fur for a homesick younger student to ruffle, or their ever-patient ears to listen to complaints or grievances, or their unjudging acceptance of the most eccentric sort of teenage behavior. ("You dyed your hair blue and are blasting Nine Inch Nails through your Walkman while studying physics? Fine. I'll be lying over here taking a nap. Try not to make any unusually jerky moves.")

Careful observation revealed that in fact our dogs worked, and probably worked even harder than the ordinary family dog, especially when you consider that they were surrounded by 340 young people. In fact, the dogs seemed to assign themselves specific duties; they had their specialties. Some dogs wandered regularly through the admissions office, or lay out in the hall, breaking the ice, giving visitors, especially shy ones, something to talk about; others wandered the campus or stood by coaches on the fields, rode in the launch at crew practice. Others were always in attendance at dorm meetings, especially those that featured a snack. One had the odd sense that the dogs almost deliberately adopted various roles, and saw themselves as essential and active participants in the life of the school. The old saying, never more

true than at the school, is "Every dog needs a job."
It was obvious that most of the dogs had found or
created a job, and more often than not, the job was
something that contributed to the life of the
community.

Of my three poodles, one male was an elderly
chap for whom the school was a kind of old-age
home. Kind and grandfatherly, he shuffled around
slowly and engaged himself mostly in putting his
top-knot under willing hands to be scratched and
petted, or in yodeling back at students who found
that he would respond to a weird kind of singing.
The second male, Louis, large, black, dominant,
principally concerned himself with making sure
everyone knew that he was the alpha dog on campus.
He patrolled the boundaries, chased interloping
dogs, played in an avuncular but concentrated way
with puppies, and only occasionally indulged his
roguish poodle sense of humor. He was once spotted
running quickly and silently up behind a family
visiting from India. When he reached them he leapt
into the air, passing them at about shoulder level,
baring his teeth. By the time they screamed and
grabbed for each other, saris flying, he had landed
and dashed around the corner of the building,
closely followed, I might say, by his master who
was yelling, "I saw you, you bad dog!" I have no
idea what the family thought about either the dog
or the owner, but I wonder if their children,
potential students, considered us very seriously.
Poodle owners know that the repentant dog, sitting
humbly, ears down, being rigorously chastised, was
probably grinning to himself. The third poodle died
of a chronic disease at age five; he had not had time
to mellow. His behavior was akin to the teenagers

of whom I've spoken before. That is, he was "a good dog who did stupid things."

My most recent dog, Folly, fairly grown up when she was introduced to campus, set herself to be a kind of guide and welcoming dog for visitors. As the constant tours came by the classroom she would leap to her feet and walk to the door to greet them. Since she loves children she was particularly careful to move slowly and carefully and maneuver her broad back to present it most invitingly to their hands. She would move to each member of the family and sniff them (as we know, also checking out the kind and quality of their dog ownership skills). She would wait until they left before coming back into the classroom and lying down, always giving me a keen look to make sure I appreciated the faithfulness and quality of her work. Before each class she would allow one or two students, always different ones, to pet her. Then she would lie down under the desk and doze off, except for the times she would lie in the middle of the classroom, front legs crossed elegantly, staring into space, only to reveal by a loud bark and howl that she had been checking out the elm tree branches outside the window for the presence of squirrels. A sixty-pound poodle leaping up and barking in the middle of class will wake up the most somnolent student. When she was a younger dog, Folly also sat every morning in the exact center of the campus circle during the chapel service, waiting to greet me as I walked out as if I were her long-lost friend. All my dogs made a job for themselves and enjoyed every minute of their time on campus.

If "every dog needs a job" applies to this most familiar human companion, the same motto applies to people of any age. Every kid needs a job. My dogs made no distinction between work and play, and healthy human beings often don't seem to make much of a distinction between them either. My four-year-old grandson works hard at his play, arranging and ordering his trucks and cars, focusing intently on simple video games, struggling to develop hand-eye coordination in ball games. He exercises his imagination by making up and telling stories; he carefully observes the other children in his day-care center and reports on them, analyzing their behavior from his own, sometimes rather bizarre, point of view. He listens intently to the books read to him and asks endless questions about them. It is hard to say where the play of work leaves off and the work of play continues.

Many of us who have been lucky enough to have jobs that involve working closely with others, though we are eager for vacation and the chance to do something different, are hard pressed to separate in an exact way when we are working and when we are playing. For teachers, grading papers is work, that's for sure. On the other hand, when the assignment was thoughtfully given and accepted with enthusiasm, even reading papers can have elements of expectation and fun. "How did the kids handle this one?" When it came time for me to retire and I was asked how I felt about my career of chaplaincies and teaching, the best response I could come up with was "It's been fun."

I've been lucky in my vocational life. On the other hand, even people who work in finance, most of whom are clear about working to make money, have also been known to find the chancy, gambling part of the job to be exciting and pleasurable, especially when they made the right speculation and made a killing. And in off-guard moments even the odd lawyer (the *very* odd lawyer) will admit that she finds the intricacy of, for example, drawing up a contract to have its moments of satisfaction and pleasure. Work and play are mixed in the reality of our lives; the division between them, while understandable and useful, is an artificial division that doesn't reflect realistically how we truly experience our lives.

The point is, in the same way as life was work and play for the school dogs, school is the work and play of youth. It is, or ought to be, as serious an endeavor as any job a parent holds (and ought to be given the same priority in the family). Yet, because learning, when handled correctly, engages a child in new endeavors and introduces her to new possibilities, school is also play. Think of the toddler who has watched mother, father, and siblings read (how thrilling it must be to do that for oneself for the first time!). For a child, reading contains pleasures unimagined, and the work it takes to learn how to read is play of the highest character.

Obviously schools have to play their part in this. Parents rightly complain about schools where teachers are time-servers and administrators are more concerned with their turf than with creating a place where the work of learning is honored and becomes fun.

Learning is sometimes tedious work and very difficult. Some learning needs to be done over and over again: learning vocabulary, memorizing declensions and conjugations, formulae and dates, concentrating in order to understand very difficult relationships—whether of historical events and contexts or of numbers.

While everyone faces a certain amount of
drudgery in academia, studying is more difficult
for some young people than for others. Some of us
are not genetically gifted in such a way that we
learn math or articulate ideas easily. We need to
learn those skills adequately, although we will
never be as good at them as others. My
mathematical inability was justly noted by
colleagues who would jokingly offer me an
opportunity to teach single-digit addition at the
day-care center. But the jokes stopped when I
proved unable at cross-country meets to add up the
score correctly. (I'll never forget the polite student
voice that suggested, "Usually seven plus five
equals twelve, Mr. Smith.")

So I was filled with admiration for those same
math colleagues who would take students who
shared my disability and work with them for hours
to produce adequate, even thoroughly satisfactory,
work. It took work and struggle on the students'
part, but if they were willing to put in concentrated
time, they would learn. Real teachers are like that,
and there are some in every school. They may be
"liberals" in their approach to learning or
"conservatives," but they are good teachers because
they are dedicated to their students' learning. In my
experience, whether a teacher was, in the lingo of
the trade, "subject-oriented" or "student-oriented"
didn't matter so long as the teacher was "teaching-
oriented," caring desperately that every student
understood the material. They were what we called
"school persons," people who were on the case
with us in teaching and learning together with kids.

Young people also develop at different rates of
speed. One student said to me as he began his
senior year, "I feel as if my brain was just turned

on." Others, after struggling for years, find themselves in a situation where whatever held them back has either disappeared or been modified in such a way that they accomplish academically what eluded them for so long. We forget, amidst the fires of family and adolescent life, that young people are growing and changing. Leaving home to go to school or college might mean that distance loosens the knots of family life and enables a student to accomplish what was previously impossible. Good kids change and often grow into themselves. There is also the fact that in youth the brain is physically developing, sometimes the change that that produces can be startling.

We were faced occasionally with parents (and therefore children) who think that learning should be "fun." "You should make it interesting for them." These same parents don't think that their work is always interesting or fun. (Can you imagine going to the head of a bank or a construction firm and complaining that you are not having fun putting together a merger and "You ought to make it interesting for me"?) Our students can't be in competition for highly competitive colleges without at the same time bearing the burden of stress or anxiety. Learning will sometimes require a great deal of concentration, struggle, and stress which, after all, are a given in life. If students are given enough support, not pushing—this is the work of parenthood—then a victory will be gained through the struggle, even if there is not the reward, in terms of grades, that was hoped for. If parents could keep in mind that the goal is learning and that the path is hard work, then everyone would be much happier and more satisfied. Obviously, this is a difficult task. One of my daughters once said to me, "You say that all you want is that I work hard and be satisfied with my work, but I see the smile on your face when I bring home A's." Those are the ambiguities we have to work with in the culture that prevails in schools and colleges. It's good to be rewarded in the conventional ways, but there are significant and long-lasting satisfactions in doing your best.

It seems to me that we get ourselves into deep trouble when grades are overemphasized, or when the opposite approach prevails and, in the cause of "self-esteem," achievement is downplayed. Kids are not really fooled by being rewarded when they haven't achieved; in fact, most kids feel that they are being made fools of, condescended to. The other side of that coin is the well-known fact that motivation grows from self-esteem. Tailoring the emphasis on either achievement or self-esteem is a difficult job. That's why we give it to adults, to parents and teachers, because they are the ones for whom the most difficult jobs ought to be reserved.

Fads are a constant in education. When I arrived at my school, there was an area on a lower floor in one of the buildings where brightly colored partitions and cubicles had been pushed together in a corner. When I asked what it was, a colleague sighed and said, "The remains of teaching machines," one of the fads of the early 1970s. Upstairs were the remnants of a "language lab." These gadgets were the bright ideas of theorists and administrators over the years, some of whom following the gleam of fool's gold, that machines that could be amortized over the years would replace expensive (and sometimes bumptious) teachers. Experience teaches us that nothing replaces a teacher, a human being who inspires and leads a student through the work, sharing the blood, sweat, and tears of the process.

Teachers are fond of the perhaps apocryphal story told of the "modern" school head who, in the midst of an argument with a language teacher, predicted that she would be out of a job in a few years because equipment, particularly cassette tape recorders, could do it better and cheaper. When he was sent on his way and his office packed up, the machines were also being loaded into a truck and the teacher, a native French-speaker, was out on the lawn with her students teaching them the beautiful accent with which she spoke.

Parents, I'm suggesting, should be wary of the latest advance that will make everything easy and new (and save a lot of money in teacher salaries besides). There are certainly lazy teachers and careless teachers, even dumb teachers, but nothing replaces a teacher. Nothing replaces the sensitivity and devotion, the do-anything-to-teach-this-kid attitude of a real teacher, and the feeling with or the empathy of, a real human being. If there is a school in your area with some teachers who are like that, then do everything you can to get your child into that school. While I spent more than forty years as a college and secondary school teacher, I never felt I had the same elegance of calling to that work as so many of my colleagues. I know that they were not unique, that there are many, many dedicated teachers in our country, some of whom need only to be set free to do the job they have been called to do so well.

Once again, the theory out of which a teacher works doesn't matter as long as the teacher is not teaching the theory but teaching the material. Remember my student who said, "There's Mr. B.

He's really easy and you learn a huge amount"? I used Mr. B. as an example, though I could have named any number of people, including the teacher of whom an excellent student said, "I have to say that I really didn't really know what it meant to work until I had Mr. T." Mr. T. is famed for being very hard, but also for leading students into what it really means to work, and therefore also into the real satisfaction that hard work brings.

So if a student comes home from school with complaints, it's important to listen carefully. In the first place, young people will often relate at home a different experience than the one they seem to be having at school. Teachers sometimes don't recognize themselves in these descriptions because home is, after all, the place where you let your hair down. All the negative feelings that can't come out at school (Do people act the same about the workplace?) flow out at home. It's important to listen through to the end of the story. Often, after a litany of complaints that make a parent's stomach drop through the floor, a student will say, "But I love my school," and wonder how his or her parent could have gotten another impression. Students need support and will get it in whatever way they can. The support is what is important—support and the hopeful opening to the future, "We know you're doing your best. Just keep at it; things will work out."

And if they don't work out, what then? It's easy for adults to say that we all face disappointment and have to learn to deal with it. With our good kids, it's often harder for the adults who also need to keep up an appearance of optimism. What's important, when school, athletic, or personal disappointments come, is for us not to put a good face on what is sometimes fairly devastating, but admit the reality and stand by the young people as they figure it out for themselves. Kids don't really need to be told how to handle things; they do need someone to stand by them, affirm the reality, and stick with them through a hard time.

One year I went with our rowing team to an international regatta. Although the team had showed promise during the season, they had actually not put it together until the late spring. So whether they would fare very well in another country, in another configuration of boat (in rowing terms, in an eight instead of a four), was a real question. In the event, the team performed remarkably well and, to everyone's great joy and even amazement, made the finals of this world-famous competition after four days of hard races against some of the best high school crews in the world. It was unbelievable that a crew, especially this crew, could come this far. They stood on the verge of greater success than any crew in the history of the school and of achieving great honor in the world of rowing. But in the finals of the event, they lost.

After the race was over, the parents who had come to see their sons row trudged to the area where boats were taken from the water, they wanted to be there when the boys (and the girl coxswain) arrived. The kids were obviously shaken and horribly disappointed, close to tears in some cases, in tears in others. (Good kids, especially boys, have learned to cry in the past few decades, taking the dangerous step of allowing themselves to feel, one of the things than makes them good kids.) The parents rushed toward the team with all kinds of solace; after all, the other team was much larger, from a much larger school, etc. (All of this was, by the way, true. My pride in them causes me to break my narrative to point out that they were outweighed by nearly eighteen pounds a person, which made this loss less of a surprise than it might have been.)

Reassurance of that kind was of course my inclination as well, but when I took the hand of one of my young friends and looked into his eyes, dull with fatigue, pain, and disappointment, I could see that solace was not what was called for. I used a common teenage vulgarism, useful, it seems to me, in small quantities and with restraint. Useful because it says in our culture what nothing else can say. "It sucks," I said, and meant it. "Yes," said the boy, as usual being more dignified, respectful, and correct than I, "it really does." And how could one take the hand of the diminutive and inexperienced coxswain, her eyes brimming with tears, and tell her that it was really all right, that they had tried their best and achieved greatly? All these things were true, but it was not yet time. It was wound-licking time. Once again the response was, "Oh, thank you for saying that." The tears flowed free, as they needed to.

There's no reason to rush to console. The pain and grief of failure, to use the word no one likes to use, but which describes a situation such as this, or an academic disaster, being cut from a team, the failure of a personal relationship, or even an act, performed by a good kid, so stupid that it brings the strongest condemnation from the adults in a school community, needs to be felt, lived through. ("O God," more than one student has said, "how could I have been so stupid? What a screw-up.") The inclination of parents is to defend or rationalize, but most young people see through those efforts and only want their parents to let them have the dignity of failure.

When one of my students was caught smoking marijuana (stupid!), I asked him after the inevitable disciplinary response, how he was. "Oh, OK," he said, "it wasn't too bad. People have been pretty nice." And how about your parents?, I asked. "Yeah, well, they're cool. They didn't like it, but it was OK." Wait a minute, I thought, what's the deal here? So I opened my mouth and blasted him. He was, and is, a young man of prodigious academic ability; but he had put into his brain a mind-altering drug in an unknown dosage. He is also a really good kid. It drove me crazy that everyone seemed to have said, "Well, that's cool. We all make mistakes." I blew up. "It's OK to take a brain like yours, treat it with a drug that changes the way it works, and not even know the dosage of the drug?"

I think he was a little shocked that his friend, the usually kindly school chaplain, whose history as a college chaplain in the 1960s had given him all too much knowledge of the culture of drugs, could lose it so completely over one joint. Somebody had to tell him the truth. OK, you experimented, got caught and paid the price, but you also ought to have learned something from it besides "That's cool."

Being a good kid doesn't give you a bye; we are all equally responsible for ourselves, especially for what we do to our bodies. Your being a good kid has largely come from the fact that older people have not only kept in touch with you, but also that they remain older people with a wider perspective and, they hope, a good bit of wisdom gained in living their lives. We owe you our opinion, sometimes expressed as clearly and even pungently as we are able. We also owe you the example of taking care of our own bodies, especially in the way we treat our brains with mind-altering substances, the most common of which is alcohol. Parents who marinate their brains with large amounts of drink can hardly criticize their progeny for using the drug of choice of their generation. Legality aside, the spiritual example is what counts.

The result of my speaking strongly to the dope smoker, as is the result in most cases where adults show their care for young people by telling hard truths and revealing how much feeling they have for the person, was that he and I are still fast friends. He knows he can trust me to "call a stupidity a stupidity," that while he is a good kid, he can be just as stupid as anyone else, including me. It's also true that my freedom to "call a spade a spade" gives him a freedom to make observations about *my* life, that are not, once in a while, without an edge. We need our friends to keep us honest, and young people are happy to engage in such a discussion, as we all know.

Being real to a good kid means the good kid gets to be real to you. It's not so bad, once you get used to it. If you don't like it when your good kid gets defensive, or shuts down and gets sullen when you exercise your critical powers, then don't get upset when the bright light of criticism is beamed on you. One of the most devastating things that can happen to a young person is when a parent who has been, by his or her own proclamation, the exemplar of moral virtue turns out to have failed to live up to that standard. One of my students once said to me, "When you've been told all your life that faithfulness in relationships is one of our highest values, and then your dad does this . . . well, that's pretty disappointing."

In fact, there is no one as happy to maintain a moral standard as a young person, especially a fairly young person. One head of a Boston school suggested that his students' harsh judgments of hanky-panky in the White House showed that they (*even* they, one could hear him saying) had moral standards. It seemed to me that this person was pandering to the very mistaken view that teenagers are essentially amoral. Nothing could be further from the truth. No one has higher moral standards than younger teenagers, mostly because they have generally never been in the position where the temptation to break a moral standard has appeared. It's easy to condemn when you've never experienced the pressure to lie, to take advantage of a relationship, or profit from a slimy act. (Younger teens can be quite slippery over the question of cheating, though, which makes the point.)

Over the years, I've noticed that older teens (around eighteen years old) are considerably less judgmental than fourteen-year-olds, perhaps because in these few short years that lie between those ages they have had more experience. The summer between the junior and senior years in high school can be a tremendously important moment as family structures of morality are challenged and perhaps replaced by a choice of personal structures, in the context of personal relationships in particular. I hope parents will be subtly alert and sensitive to this important period. It's possible at this time to have a very adult conversation about values that matter a great deal.

This is because, and to be perfectly clear about it, it is this summer that most young people for the

first time live the life they will engage in for the next
ten years or so, that is, in terms of sexual
relationships and with real opportunity to drink
and smoke. Thus one positive result of this, along
with many others, is that it is possible for them to
engage in real ethical discourse, reflecting on values
and standards in the context of the real situation of
their life. Parents might do well to be sensitive to
this moment, realizing that listening is an important
tool of teaching as much as speaking. Most young
people talk themselves through the developments
of moral principles, but they need the context, that
is, the opportunity and, what is most important, the
reflective response that an adult can give.

Maintaining that the correct decision in a given
situation is obvious—as in saying, "just follow the
rules"—is always a temptation for adults, but that
only means that there will be no dialogue or
discussion. Young people may say things with
which we disagree, and disagree thoroughly and
profoundly. That's the point! They need to hear the
disagreement, but in the context of respect for their
opinion, and with an attitude that, after all, people
can work out these differences together. This is not
the time to win an argument, but an opportunity to
say what we think, clearly, calmly, and positively,
and to give reasons for our position. A good kid is
one who has been given the autonomy to make the
decisions (anyone can make decisions, the crucial
difference is the connection with parents who hand
over the autonomy), with the dialogue and input of
the adults around her.

I know, the person who is advising this calm,
rational approach to disagreement is the same one
who a few paragraphs above went ballistic when a
good student was found smoking dope. All I can

say is that you have to know how to initiate and hold such a discussion and that I've made as many mistakes as anyone.

This sounds like a difficult task. It is—the most difficult task a parent has. You are dealing with the issue of how an individual relates to the larger society, a question over which philosophers, theologians, and politicians have puzzled for centuries. Don't underestimate the difficulty of what you are doing. You need to be wise, which doesn't come all that naturally to us. You don't need to know all the answers, but you need to be as thoughtful, direct, and careful as you can be. For most of us, that's hard, but in this life we were not, remember, promised a rose garden. That's what we say to kids; it's true for us too.

Perhaps it's a good idea to remember that "It's only common sense" is not really satisfying for teenagers or anyone. One person's common sense is not another's; what's needed is the hard work of conversation, listening, dialogue.

One of my good kid friends wrote a column in the student newspaper that was faintly denigrating to women. He was going through that tiresome period in which boys are feeling their masculine muscles, sometimes in counterpoint to the female. You would think that this stage of development would work itself out in a boy's relationships with girls, but in our culture this is often not the way it happens. You could read the column, sigh, and say, "Well, he'll grow out of that." But what happened was that his father (not his mother) spoke to him and to me on the phone. "What's this about?" the father asked. "I don't really like his attitude. Tell me where it's coming from." He was calling his son on this moral issue. What was his attitude to women

anyway? How far did it go? Was he prepared to
discuss his ideas with his mother? (Knowing his
mother, I would have advised him to hold off on
that for a week or two, maybe even a month.) The
whole incident was irritating to the boy; he knew
his father was right. But since his father didn't back
him into a corner, didn't huff and puff, his views
were heard.

Another father immediately appeared at school
after his son was caught breaking a rule for the
second time and was therefore to be dismissed. We
were wary of what we thought would be an angry
parent until he explained that the school was right.
His son had done the wrong thing, and he just
wanted to be with him. His approach to the matter
reinforced his son's developing understanding of
the limits to behavior, supported a moral standard,
and ministered to a boy who was hurt and
humiliated. Out of very stupid acts, handled with
integrity, comes a good kid.

Once again, what is needed in such situations is
wisdom, the depth of purpose and understanding
that comes not off the top of the head, but out of the
soul, or the gut. (It doesn't matter where you locate
wisdom—the liver will do—the point is that it's not
sitting on the skin or on the tongue.) The ancients
thought of wisdom as a quintessentially female
quality, even as one of the ways through which God
approaches us and we approach (and now the
female pronoun is particularly appropriate) her.
This approach is especially useful to parents who
need to spend time in preparation for such times,
not so much by reading (which is useful) or in
conversation with others (informative), but by
being quiet, reflecting, and breathing in the
presence and wisdom of God.

In the context of what we've been talking about, the question of what the student and the parent want out of school is apropos. One of my students, tired and worn at the end of the year, told me, "I wonder what this is all for, anyway." I suggested that thinking about that might be a good assignment for the summer. The value of a long, lonely walk on a beach, or through a city, or on a drive is that there is time, valuable empty time, to be alone and think. Young people need to be alone and to reflect. They are bombarded by ready-made opinions and attractive clichés, but they need, more than ever in this media-driven society, to think for themselves.

One of the issues that comes up with schools is how much emphasis a school ought to put on the development of athletic ability. Everyone knows that the lure of making a great deal of money in professional sports draws many parents into pushing a child into sports. It is also true that most young people enjoy sports. In fact, I've discovered that even kids who are not athletically talented can, if they're coached correctly, come to like sports. Kids like the ramming around, the camaraderie of the team, the rush and excitement of competition, getting hot and sweaty.

One of my beginning runners, a young man who would go on to have the highest grade point average in his senior year at a prestigious college, started off on a long run on a moderately warm day wearing a sweatshirt. When I cautioned him that heat was very dangerous, he pointed out, somewhat imperiously, "I really don't sweat that much." When he returned the sweatshirt was black with perspiration. I couldn't help but point out (casually) that perhaps the reason he thought he didn't sweat much was because he'd never done anything that might have produced that much sweat. Later, his father thanked me for introducing him to something difficult that he couldn't do perfectly, and for teaching him that physical sweat could be almost as satisfying as intellectual sweat.

Young people often don't like the overemphasis on winning (nothing wrong with winning, something very wrong with regarding winning a game as the be-all and end-all of life). One of my student friends, an excellent soccer player, said "I hate to lose. You have to pretend to be bummed out all that night." Very few kids like it when their parent becomes too involved, as if it were his or her game. My school built a beautiful athletic center a few years ago and opened it up to the surrounding community when it wasn't being used by the school. We were astonished by the behavior of some of the parents of the young athletes whose teams used the facility, and even more astonished when the police had to be called several times to break up fights between parents, whose physical violence was so serious that officials and other adults could not control it. Something is very wrong when that is the example parents give.

There are also young people who don't really care for certain sports. I don't think they ought to be made to feel that they are weird or outcasts. People are different and there is usually some sport a child likes, is reasonably good at, and fits their talents and temperament. If hand-eye coordination is absent, or contact sports are distasteful, then there are other sports. Thus, by the way, are many runners made, not born.

A good kid is an active kid, engaged and involved at a level appropriate for that individual.

It occurs to me that the parental attitude should be less to urge the child to take part in sport than to give permission in a fairly aggressive way. Sports, of all kinds, are good for kids. One coach suggested that it was good for young people to learn that they can be hurt (not seriously but momentarily, as in being tackled in football) and that it will go away and they can go on. Like all things, this is true within reason.

The famous mother who runs onto the field to comfort a hurt player may have been replaced by the mother who screams for her child to be more aggressive. There are still plenty of mothers and fathers, though, who are overprotective. After one cross-country race, a mother rushed to her son to throw a jacket around his shoulders, as if, in his overheated condition, he needed warmth. The look he gave her and the coach's response meant that it was probably the last time she did something like that! As a cross-country coach I tried to remember, when parents showed up at meets, that most parents hadn't seen a runner at the end of a three-mile race. I made sure to explain to them that their son or daughter would look pained but was really all right. Occasionally I forgot until the last minute and found myself in front of a group of gaping parents yelling, "Have you ever seen a race? He's going to look like he's dying! He's not!" The parents would nod their heads uncomprehendingly. A few minutes later they would know what I meant. Most were smart enough to leave their heaving, panting, sweating, occasionally agonized, progeny alone for a few minutes. Presto, in a few minutes the kids would be fine. Youth is a wonderful thing. Overprotectiveness is particularly tempting for parents who haven't participated in sports themselves. I suppose one might also say that overprotectiveness about academics or personal relationships is also particularly tempting for parents who haven't had strenuous experiences in those areas either.

One reason why sports are an important component in the life of a good kid is that kids learn in sports to deal not only with failure, but also with success. I know that's the reversal of the usual way it's put, but in our culture winning is such a big issue. Parents will need to figure out their own attitudes about achievement and success and the role they play in their own lives long before they deal with their children in the context of winning and losing in sports. To be a good, modest winner who shares the credit and is genuinely gracious to the opponent is as important as being a good, disappointed, stalwart loser who accepts part of the blame, if there is any to be shared. Nothing is more unattractive than a young person who blames everyone else for a loss, or worse, openly blames a fellow athlete. I think parents need to be alert to negative attitudes and address them when they appear. No one likes to lose—"It sucks"—and there's no reason to put a good face on real disappointment, but it's only a game. Learning to win as well as to lose is an important part of being a good kid because, let's face it, most good kids do more winning than losing.

Good kids will be allowed to choose what sport they like, to be engaged as deeply as they want. They will understand that their parents want them to exercise and build their bodies, want them to have the fun of competition, learn the important things that are to be learned from athletics, but that competition is for their sake and for the sake of their team and not for their parents. There is not a moral absolute about winning. A good kid, remember, is not a perfect kid.

The same thing is true with after-school jobs. We all know that it's good for kids to have a job, to learn the importance of being reliable, trustworthy, and responsible, that it's good to work hard and produce a good product or service. However, when academic work or athletics or social life are diminished because of a job that serves only to provide money for a car, for example, it seems to me that holding that job is questionable. Store owners point out that the kids who work for them are often not the young people who need the money particularly, but those who just want something extra. School is the work of young persons; they really don't need two jobs.

Guiding a child through school is one of the most difficult jobs a parent has; it takes wisdom and strength and prayerful consideration. Such prayer waits on the wisdom of God, which leads to strengthening relationships. School is the primary way for a child to grow through his or her life outside the family. It is a vital experience, meaning that it can give life, abundant life, which is part of God's promise to us all. Engaged, thoughtful, wise parents will provide a solid base from which a fledgling can take off, and a safe place to which they can return, changed—changed utterly, in the words of Yeats, until "the terrible beauty" which is a new person is revealed. Through school a young person, in the words of another poet, T. S. Eliot (though he is speaking in another context), is "preparing a face to meet the faces that you will meet," gradually building that self in relationship, which is the foundation of a healthy, spiritually strong person.

Sex and the

good KiD

A good kid is sexy. This bald statement comes as much of a shock to most parents just as the thought that their parents might be sexy comes as a shock to most young people. ("My folks? Are you kidding?" "Where did you think you came from, kid?") A good kid is closely in touch with his or her sexuality because parents have given permission for those feelings to be openly acknowledged, even though many kids would rather that adults keep their disgusting thoughts to themselves. A good kid acknowledges that sexuality is a part of life, and while expressing sexuality can sometimes be a chancy matter, the fact of sexuality can't be denied or ignored.

When the film *Good Will Hunting* came out, there was considerable discussion of the plot in one of my ninth-grade classes. There had been a "surprise" holiday. (These holidays were surprises mostly to younger students and faculty. Older students, through an alchemy known only to them, and also through assiduously cultivated contacts, were well aware days in advance.) Students had flocked to Boston and a local mall to shop and to catch up on the latest movies. Everyone had enjoyed seeing "Good Will" which was the cool film of the day and several class members waxed enthusiastically about it. After one appreciative comment by a young woman, I said, laughing, "And you also admired the handsome star, I suspect." She turned bright red and said, "Mr. Smith, I can't believe you'd say something so embarrassing in front of everyone."

Since the point of the exercise had been to relax the class before plunging into the somewhat tedious subject of the day, I was mortified not only because my plan for the period had been subverted, but also because I didn't really wish to embarrass one of my students. I apologized publicly and later, privately. A couple of years later the student's parents told me that I'd been her favorite teacher that year. "But I embarrassed her in front of the class," I protested. "We never heard about that; what we heard about was how funny you were," they said. This good kid had gotten over my assuming that she was probably attracted to a handsome young man as she grew into accepting her sexuality (and took another look at Matt Damon).

A good kid is sexy because human beings are sexual. Sexuality is an essential part of all of us, and never more so than when we are discovering it for the first time. And despite what younger young people may say at one moment or another, "Yuck, disgusting!" they soon come to an appreciation of the important role that sexuality, together with its pains and pleasures, longings and frustrations, will play in their lives. Among the battles they have to face is that there is still a steady undercurrent in our society which is puritanical and in denial about sex; at the same time, our culture is full of highly sexualized images and language. So if kids are confused, and if parents are puzzled about how to deal with it, no wonder. The first step in getting things together is to understand what's going on. What's going on is a confusion rooted in contradictory cultural modes.

The girl I embarrassed is an example of denying what is so clearly there, a handsome young male actor is stimulating for girls. The cultural complication, of course, is that girls of that age are often reluctant to admit in some circles (namely, when adults are around) that they are attracted to men sexually, since they have been taught that good girls don't say or think those things. Boys are almost forced to indicate their enthusiasm, but in ways that are often denigrating to women.

If I had a nickel for every time I've stood in a dorm room, sighed, and said, "I'm not going to tell you to take your posters down, but I'd like to say that I find them sickening," I'd be a rich man. Teachers and parents are often forced to walk the narrow path of deciding if a poster of a semi-dressed starlet crosses the line and turns a human being into a object, a piece of meat. We've found that the best way to go at this is to engage in a discussion. Many younger boys put such materials up not just because they're turned on by them, but also, and maybe primarily, to proclaim something about themselves. Discussing the disadvantages of having pictures of nearly naked women posted on the wall is a good way of recognizing what the boys are saying about themselves. "Yes, you are sexual. OK already," is our reply. (One disadvantage is that many girls are made uncomfortable by pin-ups and think boys who flaunt them are a little weird.) It also raises the question of respect for human dignity and the importance of treating people as human, not as objects. Teenagers like to make an impression on adults, but they are notoriously unwilling to discuss the issue. I have never pretended in this book that being a parent of a good kid is an easy job, and dealing with this particular issue is strenuous. The good thing about it is that most kids will forget what you say but remember your attitude. You are not censorious; you are honest, you are kind, and you are clear.

Since all the pressures of peers and society are pushing in the opposite direction, it's hard to convince boys sometimes of this moral line. And convincing is what you want to do. It's easy to say "Take it down!" though once in a while that's the only option; it's harder to help a young man or a group of young men to reason through issues of respect and decency.

One of my young friends told me that he couldn't figure out what I was talking about until he took a long bus ride in Scotland, going from the sheep farm on which he was working that summer to a large, nearby city. The bus stopped at every small town and village along the way and at each stop, looking out the window, he regarded an advertising poster that featured a semi-nude woman sprawled across the billboard. Gradually, as the ride went on he grew to recognize the commercial use of a human body and gradually, as he emotionally and morally matured over a period of several hours, he became more disgusted and turned off. He'd spent a lot of time that summer thinking about who he wanted to be. The impersonal, calculated use of this young woman's body was inconsistent with his notion of the kind of man he hoped to become. Accepting his own sexuality made him, interestingly enough, critical of the use of sexuality in a commercial context.

Our culture also leads young people to deny the varieties of sexuality. In a discussion with ninth graders, I asked if they knew any homosexuals. They denied to a person any contact or knowledge of gay people, especially one girl who kept saying, "That's disgusting! Oh, that's so awful." The rest of the group agreed vehemently. God forbid such knowledge would ever touch their minds. Suddenly one boy said, "Well, I don't know. My parents have some friends, a couple of men who are gay. They come to dinner quite a bit. They're really nice guys and my parents like them a lot; I like them." There was a moment's pause and a girl who'd been quiet said, "My aunt comes to family parties with the woman she lives with. Actually I like her friend better than I like my aunt." Then someone else chipped in with a comment about another relative, and then another family friend, and finally one of the formerly most vehement students spoke fondly of her brother who was gay.

Most of these good kids were accepting and appreciative of the gay members of their family and community when it came down to a personal relationship with them, even though they were not willing even to admit the possibility of their existence among their peers when it seemed uncool to do so. The cultural pressures were to refuse to admit any contact, when most of them had indeed had some contact. The girl who was outspoken had set the tone and parameters of the discussion—until a courageous young man reflected the truth of his experience.

A colleague used to ask her students to chart their families on the blackboard so everyone could see the various backgrounds in the class. When the student finished the demonstration my colleague would ask, "Is everyone there? Are you sure? Have you forgotten anyone?" In almost every case the student would say, "Well, there's also Uncle X, or Aunt Y, Cousin Z, but we don't usually talk about them." Someone who was not "normal" or usual had been left out, and therefore the family portrait, which was of a trimmed and spruced up "normality," was skewed. There are no "normal" families, as I've said before; every family has some people who don't fit into the very unreal picture of two-parent, heterosexual, suburban family. A good kid has learned that there are all kinds of people in the world, and they're worth getting to know before she makes judgments. Many young people don't have much experience of the varieties of people and when they do gain some knowledge of the world, they find that the stereotypes present a very false picture of what is real.

Many parents are concerned about pornography either on-line or in printed form. I have no brief for pornography and certainly no need to defend it, but it does seem to me that adults ought to face the reality of the ubiquity of pornography in our culture, not only what is produced consciously as pornography but also the advertising that uses sexual titillation and arousal to sell a product. This pornography (which is what it is) is regarded as perfectly ordinary and normal. It's not OK for kids to have lustful pin-ups in their rooms, but it is OK to use a naked woman to sell tires.

While we might be chagrined that the promise of the Internet has been subverted to the extent that a good portion of it is used for pornography, we still have to admit the reality, if not the desirability, of it. Parents and teachers waste a lot of time worrying about whether their children can access pornography. The fact is that most of them, especially older teenagers and especially boys, have seen a good deal more of it than their parents and teachers ever imagined

Half a century ago, boys passed around smudged, mimeographed pornographic comic strips and snickered over them. Today they gather around a computer at a friend's house, and make a few keystrokes to access a world of sexually provocative materials, some of it quite remarkably unpleasant. It is obvious that films and television programs are far more explicit today than they ever were. Our culture is so inured to shock that the borders of what is appropriate are pushed farther and farther away to the point that young people discuss seriously whether they are desensitized to violence and violent sexuality. They are often as aware of the issue as their parents are.

The point is that this is less a matter of restricting access than it is of educating young people to make their own moral decisions about such degrading material. We are past the time when children can be "protected" from pornography from the outside; the decision against the violent and degrading use of human beings has to come from the inside. This is another area where there is no better answer to the issue of humans using human beings than that communicated through the wisdom and love of parents and other adults. Blocking computer applications is fine if that is what parents want to do, and certainly younger children should not be exposed to materials about acts and situations they can not possibly understand, but the appropriate response to pornography is, once again, the difficult response: discussion, empathy, honesty. We always want a magic pill, a computer program, a law, when what's required is a parent, teacher, or mentor.

Curiosity about sex is one of the enduring aspects of growing up in every culture. Perhaps we ought to think more about what kinds of exposures to sexuality young people have than about "protecting" them from it. It's very hard to protect young people from any aspect of reality. The media culture of our time has made sure that they have seen more images of almost every human situation than any of us can imagine. One can protect teenagers from accessing pure pornography sites on the Internet, but we think nothing of their watching MTV and VH1. Parents ought to take a look at those channels once in a while, and see everything their children are watching. They should also be aware that their kids are also seeing whatever their older brothers and sisters and their friends have brought home. The solution is less to censor than to inculcate healthy sexual attitudes at the earliest possible age. That begins in the most minimal way, with using the proper terms for body parts from the beginning and being open and respectful about all kinds of responsible sexuality. There's also nothing wrong with having a sense of humor about sexuality, acknowledging that human sexuality is susceptible to the same kind of absurdity and silliness that is a part of all of human life. It's important that we bring our God-given sense of humor to sexual discussions with our kids. When we can laugh, even about serious subjects, our kids sense that we are comfortable and confident in the discussion.

Most young people grow through the period when they find pornography to be interesting. Let's admit that it's quite difficult to be continually inventive in that area. Once basic curiosity is satisfied—this goes with that, and then this happens—there's not much that is particularly new or different.

A good deal of heterosexual pornography involves the denigration of women, which is a real danger to boys, and also therefore to the girls with whom they are close, given the sometimes negative attitudes toward women in society. The parent I mentioned before who was so concerned about the content of an article his son had written because of its misogynist attitudes was guiding that good kid in a healthy direction. If he'd discovered pornography in his son's room, he would undoubtedly have had a quiet talk about it, not based on whether it was "dirty," but on what it said about his son's attitudes and ways of relating to women. As I've said, a good kid is not one who does nothing wrong; a good kid is learning how to be trustworthy and respectful of people and perhaps stumbling along the way. The way to deal with attitudes toward sexuality is to make sure that there is plenty of conversation about this most essential and natural activity. If that is difficult for some parents, then they must pull up their socks and get on with it.

A young person is, above all, healthy, lively, active. We know that a good deal of that liveliness is an expression of sexual energy. Most people have not lived in a boarding school as I did for over twenty years. Three hundred and forty young people can generate a lot of energy which, most of the time, is fun and enlivening, if somewhat tiring. However, a family can expect that as children grow older the hormones begin to kick in. (If I were to be somewhat indelicate, I could tell you that you will know when that is happening by using the sense of smell.) They are devoting a good deal of time and thought to sex. One study of college students revealed that more than twenty percent of the time they were thinking about sex. That study was done, by the way, while they were attending a lecture! One can only imagine what's going on the rest of the time. Well, we don't have to imagine it, because we have all been adolescents and we know perfectly well what's going on.

I am making here a plea for accepting the reality of sexual expression among young people without their letting go of the moral impulse that calls them to an empathetic response, caring about other people's feelings, treating them as we would have them treat us, aware of the power and complexity of the sexual impulse. Compassion and empathy are great tools to guide moral behavior, flawed as they can be, and parents can teach them mostly by repetition and example. It is hard for many parents these days, especially those who were raised with what are called "traditional" moral standards but which were actually ideals never realized, to identify with their children's wide emotional experience and openness to physical and sexual expression.

Young people today are often much freer with their bodies, much more likely to touch each other unself-consciously, to kiss each other, and be affectionate. For the most part they are, in my experience, very sensitive to whether this is acceptable to the other person, because sexual openness usually comes with sensitivity to the other person's emotions. The freedom young people have to express themselves physically can come as a shock to many older people. Boys are not ashamed to cry, for example, in moments of frustration and sadness, and the statistics on boys who report casual sexual contact with other boys are quite remarkable. Those of us who were raised in another generation can find this startling at first, but it's important to know more about it before making a judgment. One friend, shaking his head, pointed out to me that in his time one of the benefits of being on a sports team was that you got to hug other men. I replied that when I was in high school, I was in the band and we certainly didn't lay a finger on each other.

Most boys are perfectly aware of the difference between true friendship and taking advantage of someone. It all depends, as one young friend said to me, who's touching you and in what context. What could be violation in one context and with one person is not in another. Kids almost always know the difference, just as adults do, and kids and adults can also make mistakes. We can sense when writing or images are solely for the purpose of titillation, when something is pornographic, in much the same way young people sense the difference in physical contact. My observations over the past forty years lead me to think that the freedom of physical expression, which is a mark of younger people, has been, for the most part, healthy, and offers the promise of a generation more respectful of other people in a deeper way than was possible before. The decision to touch someone or not, with the reasoning and the empathy that goes into it, is the responsibility of all people, lending even more dignity and solemnity to our humanity.

Our culture has freed itself to think about sex consciously. This is probably the difference between the late twentieth century and earlier periods. That is, the same thoughts are going on, and indeed, the same sexual activity, but they are being openly admitted now. This creates, among other things, a new spiritual situation regarding sex, namely the recognition that all aspects of our life are a part of our spiritual life, our life with God. Many people, perhaps most, whose work is not professionally religious, find it hard to relate the sacred and sexuality—except for the assumption that religion must be opposed to sex. It hardly makes sense that the one who created all this, the one whom we call the Holy One of Blessing, did not also create the sexual part of us, and not just the sexuality that leads to the creation of children, but also the sexuality that leads us to enjoy our bodies, to take pleasure in them, to give pleasure to others, and above all to use sexuality as a way to explore and share love with other people. When Mary Gordon wrote her wonderful novel *Spending*, some reviewers and readers were shocked that a writer who was known for her sensitivity to religious issues could write a wonderfully funny, sensual book that featured a woman protagonist who enjoys sex and lots of it. One had a sense that some critics were pulling up their skirts, goodness me. But we must ask why shouldn't a writer close to the mystery and wonder of the creator be also close to the mystery and wonder of sexuality? Doesn't that make sense? Unfortunately, our theological history has meant that we give only grudging acceptance of our sexuality as a viable part of the whole of creation.

One of the spiritual challenges we face is the restoration of religious thinking that accepts the natural world, and especially our sexuality, as embodying our spiritual wonder and reflecting the mystery of God. Theologians face this challenge, but so do all of us who are called to life in the spirit of God. At least one part of this is "cleaning up" the notion of sexuality so that it is seen as fit to exist in the presence of God. Another part is "naturalizing" our spirituality so that sexuality can be part of it. Surely one of the reasons young people feel uncomfortable with religious institutions is that when they enter they feel that they must leave their sexuality behind, which is important to them because it is so new and so intriguing.

A good kid is a sexual kid, not ashamed of being sexual, not preoccupied with being sexual, as intrigued as anyone would be with something so powerful and delightful. Above all, a good kid will not regard his or her sexuality as "a dirty little secret," something to keep hidden or repress, because that will mean living life on more than one level. And there is something about the good kid that is transparent, all there.

Most good kids will find their sexuality expressed with the opposite sex. Some, an unknown number at this point, will be comfortable with the same sex, and still others will be here and there before settling down. Some students of humanity think that the third group includes most of us, except that our society has been so structured as to exclude this option and to divide us into two tribes at most. Come to think of it, most people are very seldom solely one thing or another. There are people who like sports and who are just as engaged in the arts; others who are mathematicians who are also committed musicians; still others who work at home with the family are also excellent political organizers. People are seldom either this or that exclusively; they are more often both/and.

Young people in particular are growing through various stages, their personalities are blossoming in various ways in the various stages; they are what is called volatile. You don't have to be around young people very much to acknowledge the truth of that. This means that they can be convinced that they are absolutely straight, or absolutely gay, and that this will change in a relatively short time. Most good kids have time to be here and there. There are gay people who have known that they are gay from age eleven; there are others who have come to this understanding later. The same is true of heterosexuals. Referring to homosexuality, one friend paraphrased Shakespeare on greatness, "Some are born to it, some achieve it, some have it thrust upon them." The same remark could be made about heterosexuality.

Parents will find their children's development will be like that. Just as my grandson has moved from trucks to dinosaurs, parents will find that their children will move from hanging out with one kind of people to going around with another. Young people often think that they must announce their sexuality, especially in an atmosphere where what they are and what is so much a part of them is denied. It seems to me that's fine as long as parents and everyone around them understand that this is probably, in W. H. Auden's phrase, for "the time being." Adolescents feel powerfully attracted to each other regardless of gender and tend to experiment with those feelings. A lot of that attraction is experimentation and should be taken as such. While it's possible that some experimentation might involve making mistakes that could have serious consequences, most of it is harmless.

There has been a great deal of conversation lately about gender roles. This started, in a way, when women questioned the "naturalness" of being relegated, by definition, to home and family. The discussion has ranged far afield and in such a detailed way that we need not go into it here. What ought a family to do about gender roles? Some families report their little boys seem naturally to gravitate to trucks and cars, their girls to dolls; others report this is not the case at all. Those who study the issue suggest that these differences are subtly imposed at a very early age; others point to the effect of powerful hormones on the brain. It's worth pointing out that testosterone occurs in both men and women.

I wonder if the most useful approach to this would be to suggest that a family not impose a "natural," or stereotypical, gender role on a child, but wait to see how the kid develops. We have noted before that some girls will drive their feminist mothers crazy by being fascinated by clothes and "traditional" female roles, and while some boys will throw themselves into contact sports and "traditional" male roles, others will prefer less aggressive expressions of the self. Families will find girls being aggressive in ways that are unfamiliar to some of their parents, and some boys will prefer the arts over sports. Most kids will prefer some of each.

Almost nothing bothers a kid more than having sexual orientation linked to their preference in activities. Some athletic girls certainly resent being regarded automatically as lesbian, with good reason if they're not, and artistic boys are as likely to be heterosexual as hockey players. One of the insights we seem to have gotten is that when boys are overly aggressive and troublesome, engagement in the arts can be very helpful for them. It expresses a part of them that has been frustrated. Perhaps they are reacting to that frustration in their aggressiveness. What we have learned is that athletic interest is in no way linked to sexual orientation, and people raising good kids will be careful not to confuse them by doing so. I have known gay kids who were award-winning, terrific athletes, and gay kids who wouldn't walk onto a field, court, or racecourse if you shot them. The same thing is true for straight kids.

It's important, then, in raising good kids to let them flow where they and their friends want to and not impose our ideas on them. A friend tells the story about one of his daughters who, at the time, was quite young, about nine. She was in a girls' soccer league in the town in which they lived. My friend went out to watch practice one day only to find himself called onto the field by the coach because he wanted to balance the sides. (We were quick to ask him if he'd been assigned to the stronger or weaker side.) He'd never played soccer but, being a runner, he figured he could dash around the field with ease. Once out there he took it upon himself to coach the girls and urge them to more aggressive play. As they ran down the field after the ball he suddenly felt two hands on his waist and a strong, positive shove which almost sent him flying onto his nose. He looked around with some asperity to see his daughter laughing at him, "Is that aggressive enough, Dad?" Kids can figure out for themselves the level of aggression with which they are comfortable if you give them the opportunity to decide.

Giving them that opportunity is, it seems to me, the key here—allowing the young person to experiment, to discover by themselves who they are and what fits best with their personality. One of the finest boys I know, someone who is very popular among his peers, is a quietly humorous, very tall young man who is usually seen bending over a shorter girl smiling, laughing, paying close attention to what she is saying. His father, a college basketball coach, is as eager for his son to be active in the sport as anyone. But the father has the sense to realize that this lad, who looks as much like a basketball player as anyone, will never play hoops. He is most happy and fulfilled when working hard in the ceramics studio producing remarkably sensitive and elegant pieces that take your breath away. He is a good kid and a good sport, willing to use his height and strength in another sport, though I think he's not quite as devoted to it as the coach would like.

This family has allowed their son to be the good kid he is—and he is a remarkably good one—by adapting their hopes and aspirations to who he really is. He will try out different ways of being himself, but he is doing that with the security of knowing that his family respects his individuality, and this is, once again, the path to raising a good kid. Another young woman's family sent her to school in a different part of the country because they recognized that she wouldn't be happy conforming to the norms of her native area. Her mother suggested that she didn't raise her daughter to lose tennis games because where they lived that was the accepted way for women to be. Her good kid will blossom and grow as a scientist/mathematician because that is how her mind works.

Sexuality is a difficult area for most of us. Our anxiety level rises precipitously when the subject comes up, not just on the hot-button issues of our time, but when sex is mentioned generally. This is the card we've been dealt in our society. No matter who or what is responsible for it, this extraordinary sensitivity is our lot. Parents who love and respect their bodies and love and respect other people will provide the example that speaks far more than words. Parents who keep their commitments and their faithful promises provide the security young people need to face the developing opportunities in their lives. Parents who are clear about their faults and failures and ready to face them provide an example that can be a creative power in the lives of their children. Parents who have a sense of humor and absurdity about human foibles and stumblings can give their young people a perspective that will stand them well as they face the mystery of others and the mystery of their own selves.

The

good KiD

and the

Common Good

In this book I've tried to describe rather than prescribe the way parents might set about ordering their children's growing up. I've tried to suggest that the difficult, perhaps sometimes dangerous path of waiting, reflection, and discussion is a healthy and more productive way to raise young people than to impose roles and rules. Parents need to come to terms with the fact that growing up is a process, a continuum; young people constantly change and old people do too, but at a slower rate, lower peaks, higher lows.

What doesn't change in this equation is there are, in fact, rules for life, things that are always right and wrong: one ought to be honest, faithful to a trust, true to oneself, just and fair in dealings, concerned and compassionate for the other, respectful of people, property, and the environment, engaged in one's community. It is not a very good idea to build a life solely on rule and law. Though these are good guidelines, they are better when they're considered and understood and when they're embedded in a human story, in lives that have purpose and direction and are going somewhere. Good kids' lives are largely built on relationships with others, feeling with and for other people, thinking critically and as clearly as possible about the decisions that everyone has to make, but which they are making for the first time.

I have tried to suggest that kids and the community are better off when they are allowed to grow into themselves and into their own way of handling things. We know that young people differ considerably, depending a great deal on how they are raised. The students I've referred to here are as different from each other as if they were each from different continents, yet almost everyone of them is an American.

Among these students are African-Americans, Chinese-Americans, Dominican-Americans, French-Americans and even, "Preppy Americans." Some years ago the son of a friend came home from school complaining that his family "was nothing." In his school in Chicago everyone was something—African-American, Polish-American, etc.—but his family was nothing. His mother pointed out the difficult fact that his ancestry on both sides could be traced to the Mayflower, but if he mentioned this, people would think he was snobbish or stuck up. The son stamped off, condemned to nothingness. A week or so later he arrived home from school beaming, "Mom, I found out what we are. Why didn't you tell me?" She asked breathlessly what she was. "We're preppy, Mom." He asked if he could buy the correct clothes that matched his new identity and a few weeks later arrived at school in khaki pants, a polo shirt, and loafers. So there is, apparently, such an identity as Preppy-American.

The circumstance of my experience of the past twenty-odd years has meant that I have mostly had experience with that small but vital minority mentioned above. The young people with whom I have been engaged are for the most part intellectually very able kids, some of them to a stunning extent. Many of them have remarkable resources also of money, education, and experience, especially in travel; almost all of them have had thoughtful and loving care poured out upon them. And yet, and this is the point, they have the same problems and issues as any other young person; they have all had to answer the question of identity, Who am I? and the question of vocation, What's to become of me? They are all coming to terms with these questions: Where did I come from? How has my past and my family's past affected me? How will I live into my future? Their identity has to take its stand in the world of the twenty-first century, answering not only the questions posed to us all by the challenges of our time, but also by the One who stands over all time and poses the eternal questions.

There are, besides that, the other questions which for almost all young people are mesmerizing: Will people like me? Will I make friends? Will I be successful in school, go to the college I want to go to, find the work for which I'm suited? They have needed to ask: Who am I sexually? How intense do I want my relationships to be? Are alcohol and drugs really as dangerous as the adults tell me? Can I handle them? In the end will I be satisfied with my life? No matter what position or identity one has in our society, whether one is well-off or poor, academically talented or disabled, socially at ease or ill at ease, no matter what genes or levels of hormones, no matter in what culture we are born—these are the questions that must be faced and answered, one way or another. My young friends, most of whom came from a relatively privileged background, have to deal with winning and losing, success and disappointment, with wondering and wandering. Where would they place themselves in the complex society into which they were thrown by their birth in this country? How will they act out their commitments?

Dealing with all these issues is quite a job. It isn't as though adults don't have to deal with variants of them, plus the questions and problems presented to us by marriage, child-raising, and maturity. We are accustomed, however, to swimming through these crises, and we have, some of us, a little of the wisdom that comes simply from marching through life. Young people don't have that advantage, which is why they are often distracted and stumbling, both physically and mentally. I can remember making announcements at school, looking out at a crowd of superficially very attentive young people, their eyes bright and clear (some of them nodding occasionally, as young people learn to do to indicate that they are paying attention when they are not!), and realizing through experience that probably half of them were not listening to a thing I was saying. This is commonplace with teachers; we expect kids to be thinking about something else. This is why they appear for international flights without their passports, why one sneaker can sit in a corner for a week until one of us picks it up and puts it in lost-and-found, why some desks look as though if you dug down in them you might find a family letter from Teddy Roosevelt to his son (undoubtedly saying, "And don't forget your train ticket the way you did last vacation!").

There is so much to do and to be as an adolescent, dealing with all these questions as well as the basic issues of health and well-being. It is amazing that most of them swim through these currents as well as they do. Part of the message of this book is that, in relatively steady or halting ways, people do survive and keep their heads above water, that they sometimes go under for a while, pop up again and move forward. Raising a good kid is not a momentary matter of saying the right thing at the right time and strolling away; it is not like dropping a coin in a machine. It is more a matter of suggesting, by example and consistency of effort, that the young person needs to reach into the self, which includes the imagination, to find the courage and the ability to do this business of life well.

At least one reason why young people don't hear what we're saying is that they are still working on who it is who is listening. They are sometimes someone other than the person we think we are addressing. When I drop by for dinner or a visit, my grandson is occasionally a pirate, sometimes Buzz Lightyear, sometimes Superman. My high school students, boys and girls, were grown-up versions of that. Sometimes they were scholars of probity and gravity, sometimes wild and crazy kids, sometimes sports heroes, sometimes lounge lizards. It occurs to me that occasionally I might be someone else in my mind than the person I appear to be to others. A few years ago I was about my daily summer exercise, riding my bicycle on the roads that wind through the salt water marshes in this area. I was feeling particularly good that day, and maybe even particularly good about myself. I figured I had done some good work. At that moment a chipmunk dashed out in front of me, then turned and ran back. The front and then the rear wheel of the bike went over it. There was a squeak for the first wheel, no squeak for the second. So I went from an angel of light to the angel of death in a couple of seconds. We all change identity, but almost no adults change identity as radically as teenagers.

And this is at least one reason why I think it is wise to be encouraging but a little tentative about affirming intense religious faith in young people. Knowing oneself as God knows us requires a solid knowledge of the self, of the person who is presenting the self to the Holy One of Blessing. God relates to us as we are in ourselves, not in the approved roles our society makes available to us, but as we truly are. Maturing involves the discovery of that person, and authentic intimacy with God and with others depends on that discovery. Young people, as I have said before, are volatile, always changing. They can be as much in love with God as they are with their current flame, which is not a put-down, but a realistic recognition of what's happening to them.

I'm not suggesting either that the adult personality is static; we are changing too, but less often and, with any luck, with less turmoil, *Sturm und Drang*. Just as we occasionally fall in and out of love with our partners, we also fall in and out of love with God. Not being adolescents, we are inclined to remind ourselves that this has happened before and to wait for the restoration of relationship. The faithfulness of God is surely in that God is always there, and our experience with God is "to arrive where we started and to know the place for the first time," as T. S. Eliot wrote. One of our more profound tasks as parents is to be the ones who send the young out but always to be there for them and be known by them as they change again "for the first time." Waiting, paradoxically enough, is one of the most difficult challenges involved in being the parent of a good kid who is growing into a self. We also wait as human beings who are growing and changing, although in a narrower range, not as high and not as low.

In the midst of this turbulence, we ask our kids to grow up, but we are not satisfied with that   we want them to grow up right, as good kids. Therefore we ask them to be involved with other people, not only as friends, teammates, schoolmates, but also as part of the larger community. The geographical and social organization of contemporary life has meant that many young people live in what are, historically speaking, very odd communities. I speak here of the isolation of families in the suburbs where, especially if parents are working as most must, young people have relatively little contact with anyone beyond the family (and this is often solely the immediate family, since grandparents, aunts, etc., are often in another place far removed), school, and perhaps church or temple.

It seems to me that parents might consider well the isolation of the young from the old. One of the favorite activities at my school was the community service program in which students left the isolated and isolating world of boarding school (mitigated by the young children of faculty who lived in the dormitories, and the elderly faculty, like me, who tottered about the place) to visit in nursing homes, hospitals, and schools. These lively, active kids found it relaxing and important to sit quietly with an old person who might not even remember them from visit to visit, and to listen. Used to producing, talking, working constantly, the kids enjoyed the change of pace, the change of role, all of the changes necessary in relating to the very old. Doing this exercised a part of their brains and their selves that could easily lie fallow. Volunteering challenged them to feel with people who had vastly different experiences and lives than theirs. It helped them develop their empathetic muscles that need exercise as much as any other part of the person.

Getting out of the family, having experience with people who are different, even strange, being responsible for adapting, and relating are all important ingredients of building a good kid. The understanding that might go along with this activity is that serving other people is a privilege, a chance to learn and grow, a gift that is given to them by the ones they are serving. Young people can be as self-righteous as anyone. It's important for them to see that service to others is not only expected, but also necessary to the process of building a healthy self. All the major religions understand and support this principle. My old friend Thich Nhat Hanh, whom I mentioned earlier, had been the founder of the Vietnamese Buddhist version of the Peace

Corps, recruiting young people to go to the villages of the country and serve the people there, which challenges Western ideas of Buddhist quietism.

It's important for young people to understand that in their service to others they are doing no one a favor except themselves, because the learning and development that comes from it is of inestimable value in building their personalities. My students almost inevitably found themselves moved and changed in ways they didn't expect by the people with whom they worked, whether it was the elderly, the severely disabled children in a rehabilitation unit, or the kids at the local school. The huge hockey/lacrosse player I counseled enjoyed more than he could say having tiny kids use him as a kind of tree; he also learned about the issues some of the kids faced in their families. One of my scholarly advisees had a great time dealing with the eccentric members of the local historical society, and so on. They did good work but benefited even more greatly through their contacts. Community service, sponsored by many schools now, benefits the community a little, community service benefits the students enormously, and I hope that that is made clear to them when they perform such service.

It is useful for students to become actively involved in politics on any level. This at least partially involves their parents who might become engaged and responsible in the political life of the community, expressing opinions, voting, putting signs on the lawn, no matter how much this embarrasses teenagers.

Another way that young people learn to become engaged is when parents exercise hospitality, when neighbors and friends regularly appear at the home and are greeted and entertained with the "value and worth of angels," as Paul the apostle says. Having many people in and around the house, so difficult today, helps a young person understand that he or she has more relationships than with the family, and many, many more than with friends from the neighborhood or school.

Raising a good kid means encouraging the kid to get to know people who are very different from him, for his own sake, so he will be comfortable with those who are not the same, so he will acquire the wisdom that beneath the skin people are very much alike. In important ways, and especially the spiritual, all people face the same challenges, the same questions. We believe they all face the same God.

God does not ask them or us to be any special sort of person, as the theologian and martyr Dietrich Bonhoeffer said. God does not ask them to be saints or sinners, good people or bad people. God asks them to be themselves. Purity of heart, integrity, means that we are ourselves before God. This is good enough, and hard enough. God, it seems to me, does not reach out to any special sort of person, a successful person or an unsuccessful person, the outcast or the pillars of society, the rich or the poor, intellectually able or intellectually disabled, but to every person, the ordinary common people of God with whom we live our lives. A good kid, above all, knows herself to be part of those people, sees her face, and the face of God, in all those people. The waters of life can be rough or smooth, but we are all in the same small boat—in the same Eternal Presence.

JOHN F. SMITH, an educator and Episcopal priest, has worked closely with young adults for forty years. A former chaplain and teacher at Groton School in Massachusetts, Smith helps parents step back from a fear-based approach to raising teens and encourages them to develop an appreciation of their kids. A graduate of the University of Michigan, Smith received a master of divinity from the Episcopal Theological School. The father of two grown daughters, Smith lives on Cape Cod.